T0220596

Lecture Notes in Computer Science

Lecture Notes in Computer Science

Edited by G. Goos and J. Hartmanis

78

Michael J. Gordon
Arthur J. Milner
Christopher P. Wadsworth

Edinburgh LCF

A Mechanised Logic of Computation

Springer-Verlag
Berlin Heidelberg New York 1979

Authors

Michael J. Gordon
Arthur J. Milner
Christopher P. Wadsworth
Dept. of Computer Science
University of Edinburgh
James Clerk Maxwell Building
The King's Buildings
Mayfield Road
Edinburgh EH9 3JZ
Great Britain

AMS Subject Classifications (1970): 68 C 01, 68 E 15
CR Subject Classifications (1974): 5.21, 5.27

ISBN 3-540-09724-4 Springer-Verlag Berlin Heidelberg New York
ISBN 0-387-09724-4 Springer-Verlag New York Heidelberg Berlin

Library of Congress Cataloging in Publication Data.
Gordon, Michael J C 1948-
Edinburgh LCF : a mechanised logic of computation.
(Lecture notes in computer science; 78)
Bibliography: p.
Includes index.
1. Edinburgh LCF (Computer system) 2. Computable functions--Data processing.
I. Milner, Robin, joint author. II. Wadsworth, Christopher P., joint author. III. Title.
IV. Series.
QA9.59.G.67 510'.8s [001.6'4] 79-24745
ISBN 0-387-09724-4

Printing and binding: Beltz Offsetdruck, Hemsbach/Bergstr.
2145/3140-543210

Preface

Edinburgh LCF is a computer system for doing formal proofs interactively. This book is both an introduction and a reference manual for the complete system (and its DECsystem-10 implementation). The acronym LCF stands for "Logic for Computable Functions" - a logic due to Dana Scott in which facts about recursively defined functions can be formulated and proved. The original system (developed at Stanford University) was a proof checker for this logic, based on the idea not of proving theorems automatically, but of using a number of commands to generate proofs interactively step by step. The emphasis then was on exploring the class of problems that could conveniently be represented in the logic, and on discovering the kinds of patterns of inference that arose when solving these problems. It was found that, by and large, the original logic was expressive enough, although a few useful extensions were suggested. However, the fixed repertoire of proof-generating commands often required long and very tedious interactions to generate quite simple proofs; furthermore these long interactions often consisted of frequent repetitions of essentially the same sequence of inferences.

From the experience gained, a new system - Edinburgh LCF - has been built. Instead of a fixed set of proof-generating commands, there is a general purpose programming language ML (for "metalanguage"). Among the primitives of this language are ones for performing atomic proof steps; since these are embedded in a programming language, sequences of them can be composed into procedures. Thus, where in Stanford LCF common patterns of inferences would have to be repeated, these now become programmed operations, defined once and then called many times (or even built into yet more complex operations).

ML is a functional language in the tradition of ISWIM and GEDANKEN. Its main features are: first, it is fully higher-order, i.e. procedures are first-class values and may be passed as arguments, returned as results or embedded in data-structures; second, it has a simple, but flexible, mechanism for raising and handling exceptions (or, in our terminology, for "generating and trapping failures"); and third, but perhaps most important, ML has an extensible and completely secure polymorphic type discipline. Imperative features, in particular an ability to introduce assignable storage locations, are also included; in practice, however, we have found these are rarely used, and it is not clear whether they were really necessary.

The inclusion of higher-order procedures stems from a desire to experiment with operations for composing proof strategies. Such strategies are represented by certain types of procedures; if ML were not higher-order, we would not be able to define many natural operations over strategies. Since strategies may fail to be applicable to certain goals, we also needed a mechanism for cleanly escaping from ones inappropriately invoked, and this led to the inclusion of exception handling constructs. These constructs have turned out to be both essential and very convenient.

The reason for adopting a secure type system is best seen by comparing the treatment of proofs in the present system and its predecessor. In Stanford LCF, a proof consisted of a sequence of steps (theorems), indexed by positive integers, each following from previous steps by inference. For example, if 50 steps have been generated, and the 39th step is

]- for all x. F

(for some logical formula F) then the command

SPEC "a+1" 39

will generate, by specialization, the 51st step as

]- F[a+1/x]

(i.e. F with the term "a+1" substituted for x). In Edinburgh LCF, instead of indexing proofs by numbers, theorems are computed values with metalanguage type thm, and may be given metalanguage names. (Other metalanguage types are term and form(ula) - e.g. "a+1" is a term, and "for all X. X+0=X" is a form). Thus if th names the theorem

]- for all x. F

the specialization rule may be invoked by the ML phrase

let th' = SPEC "a+1" th

which constructs a new step and names it th'. This change, whilst not profound, is very influential - the identifier SPEC now stands for an ML procedure (representing a basic inference rule) whose metalanguage type is (term->(thm->thm)), and it is a simple matter to define derived inference rules by ordinary programming.

There is nothing new in representing inference rules as procedures (for example PLANNER does it); what is perhaps new is that the metalanguage type discipline is used to rigorously distinguish the types thm, term and form, so that - whatever complex procedures are defined - all values of type thm must be theorems, as only inferences can compute such values (for example, since the type system is secure, the value "1=0" of type form can never aquire type thm). This security releases us from the need to preserve whole proofs (though it does not preclude this) - an important practical gain since large proofs tended to clog up the working space of Stanford LCF.

The emphasis of the present project has been on discovering how to exploit the flexibility of the metalanguage to organise and structure the performance of proofs. The separation of the logic from its metalanguage is a crucial feature of this; different methodologies for performing proofs in the logic correspond to different programming styles in the metalanguage. Since our current research concerns experiments with proof methodologies - for example, forward proof versus goal-directed proof - it is essential that the system does not commit us to any fixed style.

Table of Contents

Preface

How to read this document

Acknowledgements

Table of contents

CHAPTER 1

Introduction

LCF stands for "Logic for Computable Functions". As with many acronyms, it has now (for us at least) come to denote rather more than it did at first. The purpose of the machine-implemented system LCF, which is described completely in this document, is to explore both the expressive and deductive power of a particular logic and the pragmatic problems which arise in conducting proofs in it.

These two aims are to a large extent independent. Pragmatic questions, concerning styles of conducting proofs interactively with a machine, do not vary greatly with the choice of deductive calculus. In principle, we could have given the user the power to specify this calculus with complete freedom. However, any very general system is liable to yield inefficient treatment of particular cases, and we have preferred to orient our system towards one particular calculus called PPLAMBDA (Polymorphic Predicate \-calculus; the reader must get used to "\" standing for "lambda" in this text). We will come back to this calculus, and its relation with programming, later in the Introduction; first we want to discuss the pragmatic matters which motivated the design of our system.

Two extreme styles of doing proofs on a computer have been explored rather thoroughly in the past. The first is "automatic theorem proving"; typically a general proof-finding strategy is programmed, and the user's part is confined to first submitting some axioms and a formula to be proved, secondly (perhaps) adjusting some parameters of the strategy to control its method of search, and thirdly (perhaps) responding to requests for help from the system during its search for a proof.

The second style is "proof checking"; here the user provides an alleged proof, step by step, and the machine checks each step. In the most extreme form of proof checking each step consists in the application of a primitive rule of inference, though many proof checking systems allow complex inferences (e.g. simplification of logical formulae) to occur at one step. One feature of this style is that the proof is conducted forwards, from axioms to theorem; in automatic theorem provers the built-in strategy is usually goal-directed (traditionally this has been achieved by providing the negation of the goal-formula as an extra "axiom" and endeavouring to generate a contradiction).

There are no doubt many ways of compromising between these two styles, in an attempt to eliminate the worst features of each - e.g. the inefficient general search strategies of automatic theorem provers, and the tedious and repetitive nature of straight proof checking. The main aims of our system are as follows:

(1) To provide an interactive metalanguage (ML) for conducting proofs, in which in principle almost any style can be programmed, but which provides the greatest possible security against faulty

proofs.

(2) To accomodate well a particular style which we believe is natural.

(3) To experiment with ML and with this style of proof in the particular calculus PPLAMBDA, in which properties of recursively defined functions over a wide variety of domains can be quite well formulated (in particular, problems to do with the syntax and semantics of programming languages) and in which proofs are often found by one of a few good strategies, together with rather few creative steps supplied by the user.

These aims - particularly the provision of a metalanguage - arose from an earlier implementation of a restriction of PPLAMBDA carried out at Stanford in 1971-2 (see Bibliography under LCF Studies). In that system the metalanguage consisted only of a few simple commands, e.g. for doing basic inferences or for attacking goals with basic strategies. It was soon found that the ability to compose these commands into complex inference rules and strategies would be a key factor in developing a more powerful system.

There are three important elements in our proposed "natural" proof style. Most fundamental is the adoption of natural deduction, in the established sense of the logicians Gentzen and Prawitz. Here inference rules play the dominant role, rather than axioms as in Hilbert-type logics, and the emphasis is upon the introduction and discharge of assumptions, to avoid nesting of implications in the steps of a proof.

The second element is to use goal-directed proof procedures or recipes. When one mathematician asks another "what is your proof of X?" he often means "how do you prove X?"; that is, a formal proof, step by step, will not satisfy him nearly so well as a recipe for proof. A recipe could be something like "Induction on the length of the string, then case analysis and a use of the associativity of concatenation". Of course this is very vague; analysis of what cases? - what kind of induction? etc.etc.. But if pressed further, one may well give a more detailed recipe, still in the same style. The point is that such recipes - or strategies - appear to be built from combinations of smaller recipes (which we shall call tactics rather than strategies). It may turn out that the number of primitive tactics is rather small, and that many interesting strategies can be built from them using a (perhaps also small) number of operations over tactics. We call these operations "tacticals" by analogy with functionals.

One aim in designing ML was thus to make it easy to program tactics and tacticals. It turned out that nothing very special was needed to achieve this; the ability to handle higher-order functions was a major requirement.

The third element of natural proof style is to emphasise theory structure. Many theorems in mathematics depend on results in earlier theories; there is a natural theory hierarchy which should be reflected in the way one builds a body of useful theorems during several sessions of interaction with a computer (or with a library and a pad of paper). Theories about computation are no exception; a theorem about a program written in ALGOL will depend not only on theories of the data structures used in the program, but also on theories of the syntax and semantics of ALGOL itself. When you enter the LCF system, you are first asked whether you wish to work in an existing theory or to create a new one; in the latter case you will then state the parent theories on which it is to be based. Our examples in the next section and in Appendix 1 show something of how this works in practice. We do not regard our treatment of theories as complete; we have not considered ways of defining theories parametrically, for example. To see the use of this, consider building a theory of Boolean Algebra. One way to do it is to erect it upon two instances of a theory of Abelian monoids, with different names for the binary operation; the latter theory should therefore be parameterised on this name. We would like to use the work of Burstall and Goguen (see Bibliography) in further development of theories.

Let us now look at the relation between logic and programming, and attempt to place PPLAMBDA in this context. First, there is a strong parallel between deductive languages and programming languages; both have precise syntax, and both have a semantic theory (which is much more recent for programming). On the other hand there is a definite asymmetry. It is important and natural to make deductions about programs, and also to write programs to make deductions, but it is hard to resist the view that declarative statements and deduction are paramount; we will always want to deduce facts about programs - even those which perform deductions.

One current approach to this complex relationship is to avoid placing either programming or deduction above the other, but instead to build them together in a formal system which is both declarative and imperative. Whether the result is called a programming language or a deductive system is not important, and exponents of the approach would probably avoid both descriptions as misleading. Their point is that good programming should always be accompanied by deduction. Interesting - and very different - examples of this point of view are by Constable and O'Donnell, by Pratt, and by Rasiowa (see Bibliography).

On the other hand, there exists in the lambda-calculus a canonical calculus for algorithms (at least, for sequential algorithms). This has been shown by Scott, Strachey and their followers to be rich enough to define both the syntax and the semantics of programming languages; it may also be possible to employ it to describe hardware. Problems concerning the transformation of programs, the translation between programming languages, and the implementation of languages on computers, can therefore be expressed and investigated formally in a calculus of relations between lambda-terms. This is one of the roles intended for PPLAMBDA. At present, though this may be temporary, it seems that the integrated declarative-imperative calculi mentioned in the last paragraph are more suited to verifying <u>particular</u> programs.

In our view, both these and other approaches must be followed, to develop the theory of programming, and it is shortsighted to prefer one to the other.

1.1 A simple proof exercise.

We would like at this stage to perform some simple inferences, and show how a proof recipe may be programmed, in a calculus which should be familiar to the reader (it is, in fact, in a restriction of PPLAMBDA). We shall use only a fragment of ML. Our example will show how the type structure of ML provides a discipline which emphasises the distinction among the syntactic and other objects involved in doing proofs; it will also underline an important ingredient of our "natural" style of proof - that a theorem is not proved without motivation, but rather with some purpose or goal in mind.

Let us suppose that we are exploring the theory of Boolean Algebra, which we have named `BA` (say). This means that we have already axiomatised the theory, and perhaps proved some important theorems (e.g. deMorgan's laws, and the cancellation of negations), and we wish to extend our abilities to work in the Algebra. Part of this extension is obviously to prove more theorems; another important part is to define proof methods, or procedures, or strategies, as metalinguistic entities - that is, as functions or procedures in ML.

Our axioms will have been named, and will be accessible through these names. The system keeps them on the `BA` theory file in the form:

```
orcomm  "!X.!Y. X + Y == Y + X"
andcomm "!X.!Y. X * Y == Y * X"
ordist  "!X.!Y.!Z. X + (Y * Z) == (X + Y) * (X + Z)"
anddist "!X.!Y.!Z. X * (Y + Z) ==´(X * Y) + (X * Z)"
oride   "!X. X + 0 == X"
andide  "!X. X * 1 == X"
orinv   "!X. X + -X == 1"
andinv  "!X. X * -X == 0"
```

The exclamation mark stands for universal quantification.

Let us first conduct the proof of "-0 == 1" in the most obvious and elementary way, using the axioms `orcomm`, `oride` and `orinv`, with the inference rules of universal specialisation (SPEC) and transitivity (TRANS) and symmetry (SYM) of the equality relation ==. We show the proof first as a tree, in the style of natural deduction; this will help the reader to follow the subsequent ML session.

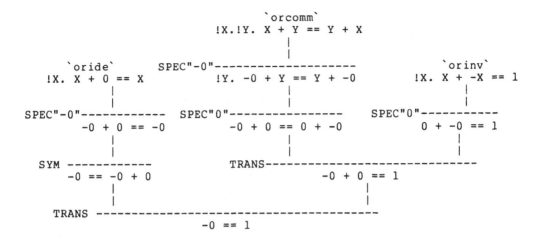

```
                              `orcomm`
                        !X.!Y.  X + Y == Y + X
                                   |
                                   |
   `oride`         SPEC"-0"-------------------          `orinv`
  !X. X + 0 == X          !Y. -0 + Y == Y + -0     !X. X + -X == 1
        |                          |                       |
        |                          |                       |
SPEC"-0"------------   SPEC"0"----------------   SPEC"0"-----------
       -0 + 0 == -0          -0 + 0 == 0 + -0          0 + -0 == 1
        |                          |                       |
        |                          |                       |
  SYM ------------          TRANS----------------------------------
       -0 == -0 + 0                              -0 + 0 == 1
        |                                                  |
        |                                                  |
   TRANS ------------------------------------------------------
                              -0 == 1
```

We will now execute the proof in ML. In each of the following
steps the user types an ML phrase after the system's prompt (#), and
the system responds appropriately.

```
*---------------------------------------------------------------*
|                                                               |
|    #SPEC "0" (AXIOM `BA` `orinv`) ;;                           |
|    ]- "0 + -0 == 1" : thm                                      |
|                                                               |
*---------------------------------------------------------------*
```

The subphrase (AXIOM...) produces the theorem]- "!X.X + -X == 1" as
its value (by accessing the theory file). The inference rule SPEC,
whose (meta)type is term->(thm->thm) , generates the theorem displayed
as the value of the whole phrase. The metatype (we shall use this
word throughout this section, to distinguish types in ML from those in
PPLAMBDA which we shall meet later) of every ML phrase is
syntactically determined, and will always be printed by the system
with the value of the phrase. Other metatypes involved in the above
phrase are term and token; "0" is a constant of metatype term, and
`BA` and `orinv` are constants of metatype token (so the metatype of
AXIOM is token->(token->thm)). Tokens are used to name theories and
axioms, and for many other purposes. Another metatype is form (the
type of formulae). "0==1" is an object of this metatype - but it
should never be an object of metatype thm; theorems are distinct from
formulae and can only be computed by inference rules. The system will
distinguish theorems by printing a turnstile]- before them.

The next step is to specialise the axiom `orcomm` to get the
theorem]- "-0 + 0 == 0 + -0" , and to combine this by transitivity
with our previous theorem (denoted by it, a metavariable which always
stands for the value of the last ML expression):

```
*----------------------------------------------------------------*
|                                                                |
|     #TRANS( SPEC"0"(SPEC"-0"(AXIOM`BA``orcomm`)) , it) ;;      |
|     ]- "-0 + 0 == 1" : thm                                     |
|                                                                |
*----------------------------------------------------------------*
```

It only remains to specialise the axiom `oride` to "-0", reverse the resulting equation by the rule of symmetry, and combine the result with our last theorem:

```
*----------------------------------------------------------------*
|                                                                |
|     #TRANS( SYM(SPEC"-0"(AXIOM`BA``oride`)) , it) ;;           |
|     ]- "-0 == 1" : thm                                         |
|                                                                |
*----------------------------------------------------------------*
```

The result may now be named `zeroinv` (say), and stored away with other interesting theorems of `BA`, where it will be accessible by the function FACT - just as axioms are accessible by AXIOM.

```
*----------------------------------------------------------------*
|                                                                |
|     #newfact(`zeroinv`, it) ;;                                 |
|     ]- "-0 == 1" : thm                                         |
|                                                                |
*----------------------------------------------------------------*
```

We shall now show how proofs may be done in a goal-directed manner. We take as goal the conversion of an arbitrary Boolean expression t to an equivalent normal form, and we consider such a goal to be achieved only by the computation of a theorem]-"t == n" , where n is an appropriate normal form.

We assume that a Disjunctive Normal Form (DNF) is a disjunction (+) of conjunctions (*) of literals, and a Conjunctive Normal Form (CNF) is a conjunction of disjunctions of literals, where a literal is a possibly negated atom (0, 1 or a variable). For simplicity we ignore the removal of occurrences of 0 and 1, and of duplicate or complementary members in conjunctions and disjunctions.

Automatic methods for our problem are of course well known, but we will use it to illustrate the interactive approach which we find natural in more complex situations. We show how partial subgoaling methods - or tactics as we shall call them - may be written, and how (in our example) they may be put together as a complete strategy for the problem.

The following is a simple recipe for converting a term t to DNF dn:

(i)   If t is a disjunction (t1+t2) , obtain DNFs dn1,dn2 for t1,t2
and form their disjunction (dn1+dn2) ;

(ii) If t is a conjunction (t1*t2) , obtain DNFs dn1,dn2 for t1,t2
and form their conjunction (dn1*dn2) , then convert this to DNF
by repeated use of `anddist`;

(iii) If t is a negation (-t1) , obtain a CNF cn1 for t1, and
convert   (-cn1)   to DNF by repeated use of deMorgan's laws and
cancellation of negation;

(iv) If t is atomic then dn is t itself.

The dual process for conversion to CNF is evident.

To formalise our recipe, we can say that our goals take the form

(t , b)

where b is the truth value true (resp. false) if t is to be converted
to DNF (resp. CNF). So we define the metatype

goal = term # bool

(**bool** is a primitive metatype - nothing to do with the subject matter
of our example). Now we can think of clause (i) of the recipe as a
partial subgoaling method - partial, because it works only on goals of
the form

(t1+t2 , true) .

We shall program it so that it escapes, or fails, on goals of
different form.   So, remembering the dual, we expect to have eight
little tactics; in fact we reduce this to seven, because the
treatment of atomic goals is identical for both values of b. Our aim
is to program these tactics separately;   later we can put them
together, and we know that this will yield a complete strategy.

Consider clause (i) more closely. It tells us what subgoals to
produce, namely   (t1, true)   and   (t2, true) ; it also tells us
informally how to achieve the original goal given achievement of the
subgoals.   More formally, in terms of inference, it tells us to infer
the theorem

]- "t1 + t2 == dn1 + dn2"

from theorems of the form]- "t1 == dn1"   and   ]- "t2 == dn2"   (it
does not compute these two theorems; that task is left to whoever
tackles the subgoals!).

This leads us to say that a tactic is something which, given a goal, delivers both a list of subgoals and a validation - i.e. a way of inferring an achievement of the goal from achievements of the subgoals. But achievements are theorems, so a validation is just a (derived) inference rule. We therefore define the metatypes

```
tactic = goal -> (goal list # validation)
validation = thm list -> thm
```

In the tactic we are considering, the validation we need is the derived rule ORCONG, expressing that == is a congruence with respect to +. It is given by

```
If thi =  ]- "ti == ui"  for each i, then
ORCONG [thl;...;thn] =  ]- "(tl+...+tn) == (ul+...+un)"
```

We assume that we have already derived this rule as an ML procedure. Now our definition of the tactic for clause (i) is

```
*---------------------------------------------------------------*
|                                                               |
|   #let ORDNFTACTIC (t, b) =                                    |
|   # if b & isdisjunction(t) then                              |
|   #  ( [(tl,b);(t2,b)], ORCONG where t1,t2 = disjuncts(t) )   |
|   # else fail ;;                                              |
|                                                               |
*---------------------------------------------------------------*
```

This is our first example of an ML phrase which is a declaration. It is likely to live on a file of useful procedures for working in the theory `BA`. It depends upon declarations both of ORCONG and of the syntactic procedures isdisjunction and disjuncts, which operate on terms.

We omit declarations of tactics ANDDNFTACTIC and NOTDNFTACTIC, corresponding to clauses (ii) and (iii); their validations are a little more complex, since they must invoke axioms and - for (iii) - some proved theorems. Three dual tactics (ORCNFTACTIC) for the CNF case are declared in the same way. Finally, the seventh tactic ATOMTACTIC for atomic goals is interesting because it produces an empty list of subgoals, so we expect its validation to be applied to an empty list of theorems. We write

```
*---------------------------------------------------------------*
|                                                               |
|   #let ATOMTACTIC (t, b) =                                     |
|   # if atomic(t) then ( [], \[].REFL(t) )                     |
|   # else fail ;;                                              |
|                                                               |
*---------------------------------------------------------------*
```

Notice that lambda-abstraction (\) is allowed in ML; in this case the prefix \[] will cause the validation to fail except when applied to an empty list. The basic inference rule

```
        REFL : term -> thm
```

(reflexivity of ==) is used; REFL(t) =]- "t==t" .

At this point the reader may be wondering when and how the
validations come to be applied, to yield the theorems we want; it
appears perhaps a rather indirect way of doing things. Here is part
of a simple-minded session at the terminal, to make this point
clearer. The user first states a goal:

```
*-------------------------------------------------------------*
|                                                             |
|    #let g =  "-(A + (-B * C))", true ;;                      |
|    g = "-(A + (-B * C))", true  : goal                       |
|                                                             |
*-------------------------------------------------------------*
```

Now he applies NOTDNFTACTIC, knowing that he will get a goal list and
a validation:

```
*-------------------------------------------------------------*
|                                                             |
|    #let gl,v = NOTDNFTACTIC (g) ;;                           |
|    gl = [ ("A + (-B * C)", false) ] : goal list             |
|     v = - : validation                                      |
|                                                             |
*-------------------------------------------------------------*
```

Now his goal list (consisting of a single subgoal: convert
"A + (-B * C)" to CNF) and his validation (which the system does not
print out, since it never prints a procedure) are bound to
metavariables.

At this point he can choose any way he likes of producing a theorem
]- "A + (-B * C) == cn" , where cn is a CNF, and submit it (in a
singleton list) to the validation v. He may choose to apply
ORCNFTACTIC to the single subgoal, or he may choose to achieve it
directly as follows:

```
*-------------------------------------------------------------*
|                                                             |
|    #SPEC"C" (SPEC"-B" (SPEC"A" (AXIOM`BA``ordist`))) ;;      |
|    ]- "A + (-B * C)  ==  (A + -B) * (A + C)" : thm           |
|                                                             |
|    #v[it] ;;                                                 |
|    ]- "-(A + (-B * C))  ==  (-A * B) + (-A * -C)" : thm      |
|                                                             |
*-------------------------------------------------------------*
```

If he had chosen to apply ORCNFTACTIC, he would have obtained two
further subgoals and a further validation, v' say; then, having
achieved the subgoals by theorems th1 and th2, he would achieve his
main goal by evaluating the phrase v[v'[th1;th2]] .

However, our seven tactics do so little work that the method must still appear a bit cumbersome. What makes it worthwhile is the ability to glue tactics together in different ways, using combinators called tacticals (as mentioned above). Only two ways are needed here. The first is alternation of tactics. Roughly, if Tl and T2 are tactics, then so is "try Tl; if that fails, try T2". It is easy to write in ML a binary infixed tactical

         ORELSE : tactic # tactic -> tactic

which represents this form of tactic composition; we have provided it as part of the system. The second way is repetition: "go on trying T on the goal and then on successive subgoals until it cannot be further applied". This is represented by the unary tactical (which we also provide)

         REPEAT : tactic -> tactic

Notice that the tactic REPEAT(T) must build a (possibly complex) validation from all the validations produced by T on the different subgoals encountered; when this validation is eventually applied, a correspondingly complex proof will be performed which the user need never see.

Now a complete strategy for normal form conversion may be declared:

```
*-------------------------------------------------------------*
|                                                             |
|    #let STRATEGY = REPEAT ( ORDNFTACTIC   ORELSE            |
|    #                       ORCNFTACTIC   ORELSE            |
|    #                       ANDDNFTACTIC  ORELSE            |
|    #                        - - - -                        |
|    #                        - - - - ORELSE                 |
|    #                       ATOMTACTIC )  ;;                |
|                                                             |
*-------------------------------------------------------------*
```

Then another way of achieving the original goal g, after its statement, is immediate and simple:

```
*-------------------------------------------------------------*
|                                                             |
|    #let gl,v = STRATEGY (g) ;;                              |
|    gl = [] : goal list                                     |
|     v = - : validation                                     |
|                                                             |
|    #v[] ;;                                                  |
|    ]- "-(A + (-B * C)) == (-A * B) + (-A * -C)" : thm       |
|                                                             |
*-------------------------------------------------------------*
```

Notice that the empty subgoal list is obtained, and it only remains to apply the validation. Of course one may augment a strategy to apply its validation automatically (to the empty theorem list) in case of an empty subgoal list; it seems misleading to do so however, since in most interesting applications complete strategies do not exist, and the task of invoking the validation on success of a strategy is more of a pleasure than a burden to the user!

No doubt the reader will have seen that a badly programmed tactic or strategy may produce validations which are nonsense; we discuss this important question in Section 2.5, where we define a notion of validity for tactics. Roughly, a tactic is valid if its validations work correctly; an important property of our tacticals ORELSE, REPEAT and others is that they preserve validity.

We repeat: LCF is secure in the sense that all objects of type thm which can be computed must be theorems, and this provides confidence in results which is not diminished by the possibility of invalid tactics.

1.2 ML.

As already suggested, ML is a general purpose programming language. It is derived in different aspects from ISWIM, POP2 and GEDANKEN, and contains perhaps two new features. First, it has an escape and escape trapping mechanism, well-adapted to programming strategies which may be (in fact usually are) inapplicable to certain goals. Second, it has a polymorphic type discipline which combines the flexibility of programming in a typeless language with the security of compile-time typechecking (as in other languages, you may also define your own types, which may be abstract and/or recursive); this is what ensures that a well-typed program cannot perform faulty proofs.

The only sense in which ML is specialized to conducting proofs is that there are types, and functions at those types, which correspond to the syntax classes of the object language PPLAMBDA and to syntactic operations over it; as we saw in our exercise above, the type thm (theorems) is distinct from the type form (formulae), and objects of type thm can only be computed by inference rules (which are ML procedures) or introduced as non-logical axioms.

For those primarily interested in the design of programming languages, a few remarks here may be helpful both about ML as a candidate for comparison with other recently designed languages, and about the description of ML which we provide. On the first point, although we did not set out with programming language design as a primary aim, we believe that ML does contain features worthy of serious consideration; these are the escape mechanism and the polymorphic type discipline mentioned above, and also the attempt to make programming with functions - including those of higher type - as easy and natural as possible. We are less happy about the imperative aspects of the language, and would wish to give them further thought if we were mainly concerned with language design. In particular, the constructs for controlling iteration both by boolean conditions and by escape-trapping (which we included partly for experiment) are perhaps too complex taken together, and we are sensitive to the criticism that escape (or failure, as we call it) reports information only in the form of a token or symbol string. This latter constraint results mainly from our type discipline; we do not know how best to relax the constraint while maintaining the discipline.

Concerning the description of ML, we have tried both to initiate users by examples of programming and to give a precise definition, and to achieve both these aims fully would probably take more space than we felt appropriate, in a document which also discusses the intended application of the language - interactive proof. We have not tried to evaluate the novel aspects of ML in comparison with other languages. Nevertheless, we are encouraged by the speed with which some users have begun to perform proofs in the system, using an early draft of this document with rather little help from its authors.

1.3 PPLAMBDA.

The terms of PPLAMBDA calculi are those of the typed \-calculus, together with fixed point combinators. Each type is interpreted as a domain which is a complete partial order (that is, there is a minimum element in the domain, and ascending chains have least upper bounds). Atomic formulae are built from terms by the binary relation symbols == (for equality) and << (for the partial order), and compound formulae are those of a predicate calculus built by conjunction, implication and universal quantification. This yields the expressive power of the full predicate calculus, since falsehood may be represented by the atomic formula "TT==FF", where "TT" and "FF" denote the two defined truth values in the three-element domain (represented by the type ":tr") whose third (undefined) member is denoted by "UU:tr".

This mention of two levels of truth - the three values represented by terms of type ":tr" versus the two values represented by formulae - needs elucidation. Terms stand for computable functions or computed objects (truth values being an instance of the latter), while formulae stand for propositions about these functions or objects. Since computations may run for ever, an undefined truth value is necessary for the interpretation of some terms.

PPLAMBDA is a family of calculi, each of which is determined by a set of types, constants and non-logical axioms. PPLAMBDA and its interpretation are discussed in detail in "A Logic for Computable Functions with reflexive and polymorphic types" (see the Bibliography) although the implemented version differs in a few practical details. An important part of its implementation, as we mentioned before, is a discipline for developing separate theories - i.e. particular members of the family - incrementally from session to session. One such theory might concern a particular programming language, ALGOL say. A theorem stating the correctness of a compiling algorithm from ALGOL to another language would belong to a joint theory - that is, to the join of the two separate language theories.

We do not claim that PPLAMBDA is adequate for all problems concerning recursive functions and programming languages. Nevertheless, it is expressive enough that, in the context of the LCF system, one may gain valuable experience in the methodology of interactive proof; this methodology is the focus of the system, rather than the attempt to find a fully adequate formalism - which is probably doomed to failure even in such a restricted problem domain.

CHAPTER 2

ML

2.1 Introduction and examples.

ML is an interactive language. At top-level one can:

1. evaluate expressions

2. perform declarations

3. begin or end sections.

To give a first impression of the system, we reproduce below a session at a terminal in which simple uses of various ML constructs are illustrated. To make the session easier to follow, it is split into a sequence of sub-sessions displayed in boxes. Each box is accompanied by an explanation of the sub-session in it; the complete session consists of the concatenation of the contents of the boxes. A complete description of the syntax of ML is given in 2.2, and of the semantics in 2.3.

Expressions.

The ML prompt is "#", and so lines beginning with this contain the user's contribution; all other lines are output by the system.

```
*-------------------------------------------------------------*
|                                                             |
|    #2+3;;                                                    |
|    5 : int                                                  |
|                                                             |
|    #it;;                                                     |
|    5 : int                                                  |
|                                                             |
*-------------------------------------------------------------*
```

ML prompted with #, the user then typed "2+3;;" followed by a return; ML then responded with "5 : int", a new line, and then prompted again. The user then typed "it;;" followed by a return, and the system responded by typing "5 : int" again. In general to evaluate an expression e one types "e;;" followed by a return; the system then prints e's value and type. The value of the last expression evaluated at top level is remembered in the identifier "it".

Declarations.

The declaration "let x=e" evaluates e and binds the resulting value to x.

```
*------------------------------------------------------------*
|                                                            |
|    #let x=2*3;;                                            |
|    x = 6 : int                                            |
|                                                            |
|    #it=x;;                                                 |
|    false : bool                                           |
|                                                            |
*------------------------------------------------------------*
```

Notice that declarations do not effect "it". To bind x1,...,xn simultaneously to the values of e1,...,en one can perform either the declaration "let x1=e1 and x2=e2 ... and xn=en" or, equivalently, the declaration "let x1,x2,...,xn = e1,e2,...,en".

```
*------------------------------------------------------------*
|                                                            |
|    #let y=10 and z=x;;                                     |
|    y = 10 : int                                           |
|    z = 6 : int                                            |
|                                                            |
|    #let x,y = y,x;;                                        |
|    x = 10 : int                                           |
|    y = 6 : int                                            |
|                                                            |
*------------------------------------------------------------*
```

A declaration d can be made local to the evaluation of an expression e by evaluating "d in e". The expression "e where b" (where b is a binding such as "x=2") is equivalent to "let b in e".

```
*------------------------------------------------------------*
|                                                            |
|    #let x=2 in x*y;;                                       |
|    12 : int                                               |
|                                                            |
|    #x;;                                                    |
|    10 : int                                               |
|                                                            |
|    #x*y where x=2;;                                        |
|    12 : int                                               |
|                                                            |
*------------------------------------------------------------*
```

Sections.

Top-level declarations normally hold for the rest of a session; to limit their scope to part of a session, sections are used. In the following we begin a section named "1.1", compute the square of 12 (using x as a local identifier) and then end the section and export the result.

```
#x;;
10 : int

#begin 1.1;;

#let x=12;;
x = 12 : int

#x*x;;
144 : int

#end 1.1;;

#let y = it;;
y = 144 : int

#x;;
10 : int
```

The top level commands "begin 1.1" and "end 1.1" begin and end the section. Notice that on ending section 1.1:

1. "it" is not effected, thus a value is exported from the section.

2. The binding for "x" reverts to that in effect when the section was begun.

Assignment.

Identifiers can be declared assignable using "letref" instead of "let". Values bound to such identifiers can be changed with the assignment expression "x:=e", which changes the value bound to "x" to be the value of e. Attempts to assign to non-assignable variables are detected by the typechecker.

```
*--------------------------------------------------------------*
|                                                              |
|    #x:=1;;                                                    |
|    UNBOUND OR NON-ASSIGNABLE VARIABLE x                       |
|    TYPECHECK FAILED                                           |
|                                                              |
|    #letref x=1 and y=2;;                                      |
|    x = 1 : int                                                |
|    y = 2 : int                                                |
|                                                              |
|    #x:=6;;                                                    |
|    6 : int                                                    |
|                                                              |
|    #x;;                                                       |
|    6 : int                                                    |
|                                                              |
*--------------------------------------------------------------*
```

The value of an assignment "x:=e" is the value of e (hence the value of "x:=6" is 6). Simultaneous assignments can also be done:

```
*--------------------------------------------------------------*
|                                                              |
|    #x,y := y,x;;                                              |
|    2,6 : (int # int)                                          |
|                                                              |
|    #x,y;;                                                     |
|    2,6 : (int # int)                                          |
|                                                              |
*--------------------------------------------------------------*
```

The type "(int # int)" is the type of integer pairs.

Functions.

To define a function f with formal parameter x and body e one performs the declaration: "let f x = e". To apply f to an actual parameter e one evaluates the expression: "f e".

```
*--------------------------------------------------------------*
|                                                              |
|    #let f x = 2*x;;                                           |
|    f = - : (int -> int)                                       |
|                                                              |
|    #f 4;;                                                     |
|    8 : int                                                    |
|                                                              |
*--------------------------------------------------------------*
```

Functions are printed as "-" followed by their type. Application binds tighter than anything else in the language; thus, for example, "f 3 + 4" means "(f 3)+4" not "f(3+4)". Functions of several arguments can be defined:

```
*-------------------------------------------------------------*
|                                                             |
|    #let add x y = x+y;;                                      |
|    add = - : (int -> (int -> int))                          |
|                                                             |
|    #add 3 4;;                                                |
|    7 : int                                                  |
|                                                             |
|    #let f = add 3;;                                          |
|    f = - : (int -> int)                                     |
|                                                             |
|    #f 4;;                                                    |
|    7 : int                                                  |
|                                                             |
*-------------------------------------------------------------*
```

Application associates to the left so "add 3 4" means "(add 3)4".
In the expression "add 3", add is partially applied to 3; the
resulting value is a function - the function of type "(int -> int)"
which adds 3 to its argument. Thus add takes its arguments one at a
time; we could have made add take a single argument of the Cartesian
product type "(int # int)":

```
*-------------------------------------------------------------*
|                                                             |
|    #let add(x,y) = x+y;;                                     |
|    add = - : ((int # int) -> int)                           |
|                                                             |
|    #add(3,4);;                                               |
|    7 : int                                                  |
|                                                             |
|    #let z = (3,4) in add z;;                                 |
|    7 : int                                                  |
|                                                             |
|    #add 3;;                                                  |
|    ILL-TYPED PHRASE: 3                                       |
|    HAS AN INSTANCE OF TYPE   int                            |
|    WHICH SHOULD MATCH TYPE   (int # int)                    |
|    TYPECHECK FAILED                                         |
|                                                             |
*-------------------------------------------------------------*
```

As well as taking structured arguments (e.g. "(3,4)") functions may
also return structured results.

```
*-------------------------------------------------------------*
|                                                             |
|    #let sumdiff(x,y) = (x+y,x-y);;                           |
|    sumdiff = - : ((int # int) -> (int # int))               |
|                                                             |
|    #sumdiff(3,4);;                                           |
|    7,-1 : (int # int)                                       |
|                                                             |
*-------------------------------------------------------------*
```

Recursion.

The following is an attempt to define the factorial function:

```
*------------------------------------------------------------*
|                                                            |
|    #let fact n = if n=0 then 1 else n*fact(n-1);;          |
|    UNBOUND OR NON-ASSIGNABLE VARIABLE fact                 |
|    TYPECHECK FAILED                                        |
|                                                            |
*------------------------------------------------------------*
```

The problem is that any free variables in the body of a function have the bindings they had just before the function was declared; "fact" is such a free variable in the body of the declaration above, and since it isn't defined before its own declaration, an error results. To make things clear consider:

```
*------------------------------------------------------------*
|                                                            |
|    #let f n = n+1;;                                        |
|    f = - : (int -> int)                                    |
|                                                            |
|    #let f n = if n=0 then 1 else n*f(n-1);;                |
|    f = - : (int -> int)                                    |
|                                                            |
|    #f 3;;                                                  |
|    9 : int                                                 |
|                                                            |
*------------------------------------------------------------*
```

Here "f 3" results in the evaluation of "3*f(2)", but now the first f is used so "f(2)" evaluates to 2+1=3, hence the expression "f 3" results in 3*3=9. To make a function declaration hold within its own body "letrec" instead of "let" must be used. The correct recursive definition of the factorial function is thus:

```
*------------------------------------------------------------*
|                                                            |
|    #letrec fact n = if n=0 then 1 else n*fact(n-1);;       |
|    fact = - : (int -> int)                                 |
|                                                            |
|    #fact 3;;                                               |
|    6 : int                                                 |
|                                                            |
*------------------------------------------------------------*
```

Iteration.

The construct "if el then e2 loop e3" is the same as "if el then e2 else e3" in the true case; when el evaluates to false, e3 is evaluated and control loops back to the front of the construct again. As an illustration here is an iterative definition of "fact" (which uses two local assignable variables: "count" and "result").

```
*------------------------------------------------------------*
|                                                            |
|    #let fact n =                                           |
|    #     letref count=n and result=1                      |
|    #     in     if count=0                                 |
|    #            then result                               |
|    #            loop count,result := count-1,count*result;; |
|    fact = - : (int -> int)                                |
|                                                            |
|    #fact 4;;                                               |
|    24 : int                                               |
|                                                            |
*------------------------------------------------------------*
```

The "then" in "if el then e2 else e3" may also be replaced by "loop" to cause iteration when el evaluates to true. Thus "if el loop e2 else e3" is equivalent to "if not(el) then e3 loop e2". The conditional/loop construct can have a number of conditions, each preceded by "if"; the expression guarded by each condition may be preceded by "then", or by "loop" when the whole construct is to be reevaluated after evaluating the guarded expression:

```
*------------------------------------------------------------*
|                                                            |
|    #let gcd(x,y) =                                         |
|    #     letref x,y = x,y                                  |
|    #     in     if x>y loop x:=x-y                         |
|    #            if x<y loop y:=y-x                         |
|    #            else x;;                                   |
|    gcd = - : ((int # int) -> int)                          |
|                                                            |
|    #gcd(12,20);;                                           |
|    4 : int                                                |
|                                                            |
*------------------------------------------------------------*
```

Lists.

If el,...,en all have type ty then the ML expression "[el;...;en]" has type (ty list). The standard functions on lists are "hd" (head), "tl" (tail), "null" (which tests whether a list is empty - i.e. is equal to "[]"), and the infixed operators "." (cons) and "@" (append, or concatenation).

```
*-------------------------------------------------------*
|                                                       |
|   #let m = [1;2;(2+1);4];;                            |
|   m = [1; 2; 3; 4] : (int list)                       |
|                                                       |
|   #hd m , tl m;;                                      |
|   1, [2; 3; 4] : (int # (int list))                   |
|                                                       |
|   #null m , null [];;                                 |
|   false, true : (bool # bool)                         |
|                                                       |
|   #0.m;;                                              |
|   [0; 1; 2; 3; 4] : (int list)                        |
|                                                       |
|   #[1; 2] @ [3; 4; 5; 6];;                            |
|   [1; 2; 3; 4; 5; 6] : (int list)                     |
|                                                       |
|   #[1;true;2];;                                       |
|   ILL-TYPED PHRASE: true                              |
|   HAS AN INSTANCE OF TYPE     bool                    |
|   WHICH SHOULD MATCH TYPE     int                     |
|                                                       |
*-------------------------------------------------------*
```

All the members of a list must have the same type (although this
type could be a sum, or disjoint union, type - see 2.4).

Tokens.

A sequence of characters in token quotes (`) is a token.

```
*-------------------------------------------------------*
|                                                       |
|   #`this is a token`;;                                |
|   `this is a token` : tok                             |
|                                                       |
|   #``this is a token list``;;                         |
|   [`this`; `is`; `a`; `token`; `list`] : (tok list)   |
|                                                       |
|   #it = ``this is a`` @ [`token`;`list`];;            |
|   true : bool                                         |
|                                                       |
*-------------------------------------------------------*
```

The expression " ``tok1 tok2 ... tokn`` " is an alternative syntax
for "[`tok1`; `tok2`; ... ;`tokn`]".

Polymorphism.

The list processing functions "hd", "tl" etc can be used on all types of lists.

```
*---------------------------------------------------------------*
|                                                               |
|    #hd [1;2;3];;                                              |
|    1 : int                                                    |
|                                                               |
|    #hd [true;false;true];;                                    |
|    true : bool                                                |
|                                                               |
|    #hd ``this is a token list``;;                            |
|    `this` : tok                                              |
|                                                               |
*---------------------------------------------------------------*
```

Thus "hd" has more than one type, for example above it is used with types   "((int list) -> int)",   "((bool list) ->"bool)"   and "((tok list) -> tok". In fact if ty is any type then "hd" has the type "((ty list) -> ty)". Functions, like "hd", with many types are called polymorphic, and ML uses type variables "*",   "**",   "***" etc to represent their types.

```
*---------------------------------------------------------------*
|                                                               |
|    #hd;;                                                      |
|    - : ((* list) -> *)                                        |
|                                                               |
|    #letrec map f l = if null l then []                        |
|    #                     else f(hd l).map f (tl l);;          |
|    map = - : ((* -> **) -> ((* list) -> (** list)))           |
|                                                               |
|    #map fact [1;2;3;4];;                                      |
|    [1; 2; 6; 24] : (int list)                                |
|                                                               |
*---------------------------------------------------------------*
```

map takes a function f (with argument type * and result type **), and a list l (of elements of type *), and returns the list obtained by applying f to each element of l (which is a list of elements of type **). map can be used at any instance of its type: above, both * and ** were instantiated to int; below, * is instantiated to (int list) and ** to bool. Notice that the instance need not be specified; it is determined by the typechecker.

```
*---------------------------------------------------------------*
|                                                               |
|    #map null [[1;2]; []; [3]; []];;                          |
|    [false; true; false; true] : (bool list)                  |
|                                                               |
*---------------------------------------------------------------*
```

Lambda-expressions.

The expression "\x.e" evaluates to a function with formal parameter x and body e. Thus "let f x = e" is equivalent to "let f = \x.e". Similarly "let f(x,y)z = e" is equivalent to "let f = \(x,y).\z.e". Repeated "\"`s, as in "\(x,y).\z.e", may be abbreviated by "\(x,y)z.e". The character "\" is our representation of lambda, and expressions like "\x.e" and "\(x,y)z.e" are called lambda-expressions.

```
#\x.x+1;;
- : (int -> int)

#it 3;;
4 : int

#map (\x.x*x) [1;2;3;4];;
[1; 4; 9; 16] : (int list)

#let doubleup = map (\x.x@x);;
doubleup = - : (((* list) list) -> ((* list) list))

#doubleup [``a b``; ``c``];;
[[`a`; `b`; `a`; `b`]; [`c`; `c`]] : ((tok list) list)

#doubleup [ [1;2]; [3;4;5] ];;
[[1; 2; 1; 2]; [3; 4; 5; 3; 4; 5]] :((int list) list)
```

Failure.

Some standard functions **fail** at run-time on certain arguments, yielding a token (which is usually the function name) to identify the sort of failure. A failure with token `t` may also be generated explicitly by evaluating the expression "failwith `t`" (or more generally "failwith e" where e has type tok).

```
#hd(tl[2]);;
EVALUATION FAILED hd

#1/0;;
EVALUATION FAILED div

#(1/0)+1000;;
EVALUATION FAILED div

#failwith (hd ``this is a token list``);;
EVALUATION FAILED this
```

A failure can be trapped by "?"; the value of the expression "el?e2" is that of el, unless el causes a failure, in which case it is the value of e2.

```
#hd(tl[2]) ? 0;;
0 : int

#(1/0)?1000;;
1000 : int

#let half n =
#    if n=0 then failwith `zero`
#            else let m=n/2
#                 in if n=2*m then m else failwith`odd`;;
half = - : (int -> int)
```

The function half only succeeds on non-zero even numbers; on 0 it fails with `zero`, and on odd numbers it fails with `odd`.

```
#half 4;;
2 : int

#half 0;;
EVALUATION FAILED zero

#half 3;;
EVALUATION FAILED odd

#half 3 ? 1000;;
1000 : int
```

Failures may be trapped selectively (on token) by "??"; if el fails with token `t`, then the value of "el ??``tl ... tn`` e2" is the value of e2 if t is one of tl,...,tn, otherwise the expression still fails with `t`.

```
#half(0) ??``zero plonk`` 1000;;
1000 : int

#half(1) ??``zero plonk`` 1000;;
EVALUATION FAILED odd
```

One may add several "??" traps to an expression, and one may add a "?" trap at the end as a catchall.

```
#half(1)
#   ??``zero`` 1000
#   ??``odd``  2000;;
2000 : int

#hd(tl[half(4)])
#   ??``zero`` 1000
#   ??``odd``  2000
#   ? 3000;;
3000 : int
```

One may use "!" or "!!" in place of "?" or "??" to cause re-iteration of the whole construct, like using "loop" in place of "then".

```
#let same(x,y) =
#    if x>y then failwith `greater`
#    if x<y then failwith `less`
#          else x;;
same = - : ((int # int) -> int)

#let gcd(x,y) =
#    letref x,y = x,y
#    in  same(x,y)
#          !!``greater`` x:=x-y
#          !!``less``    y:=y-x;;
gcd = - : ((int # int) -> int)

#gcd(12,20);;
4 : int
```

Defined Types

Types can be given names:

```
#lettype intpair = int # int;;

#let p = 12,20;;
p = 12,20 : intpair
```

The new name is simply an abbreviation; for example, "intpair" and "int#int" are completely equivalent. The system always uses the most recently defined name when printing types.

```
*-----------------------------------------------------------------*
|                                                                 |
|    #gcd;;                                                        |
|    - : (intpair -> int)                                         |
|                                                                 |
|    #gcd p;;                                                      |
|    4 : int                                                      |
|                                                                 |
*-----------------------------------------------------------------*
```

Abstract Types

New types (rather than mere abbreviations) can also be defined. For example, to define a type "time" we could do:

```
*-----------------------------------------------------------------*
|                                                                 |
|    #abstype time = int # int                                    |
|    # with maketime(hrs,mins) = if  hrs<0 or 23<hrs or           |
|    #                              mins<0 or 59<mins             |
|    #                           then fail                        |
|    #                           else abstime(hrs,mins)          |
|    # and hours t = fst(reptime t)                               |
|    # and minutes t = snd(reptime t);;                           |
|    maketime = - : (intpair -> time)                             |
|    hours = - : (time -> int)                                    |
|    minutes = - : (time -> int)                                  |
|                                                                 |
*-----------------------------------------------------------------*
```

This declaration defines an abstract (i.e. new) type "time" together with three primitive functions: "maketime", "hours" and "minutes". In general an abstract type declaration has the form "abstype ty=ty' with b" where b is a binding, i.e. the kind of phrase that can follow "let" or "letrec". Such a declaration introduces a new type ty which is represented by ty'. Only within b can one use the (automatically declared) functions absty (of type ty'->ty) and repty (of type ty->ty'), which map between a type and its representation. In the example above "abstime" and "reptime" are only available in the definitions of "maketime", "hours" and "minutes"; these latter three functions, on the other hand, are defined throughout the scope of the declaration.   Thus   an abstract type declaration simultaneously declares a new type together with primitive functions for the type. The representation of the type (i.e. ty'), and of the primitives (i.e. the right hand sides of the definitions in b), is not accessible outside the with-part of the declaration.

```
*---------------------------------------------------------*
|                                                         |
|    #let t = maketime(8,30);;                            |
|    - : time                                             |
|                                                         |
|    #hours t , minutes t;;                               |
|    8,30 : intpair                                       |
|                                                         |
*---------------------------------------------------------*
```

Notice that values of an abstract type are printed as "-", like
functions.

Type Operators

Both "list" and "#" are examples of type operators; "list" has one
argument (hence "* list") whereas "#" has two (hence "* # **"). Each
type operator has various primitive operations associated with it, for
example "list" has "null", "hd", "tl",... etc, and "#" has "fst",
"snd" and the infix ",".

```
*---------------------------------------------------------*
|                                                         |
|    #let z = it;;                                        |
|    z = 8,30 : intpair                                   |
|                                                         |
|    #fst z;;                                             |
|    8 : int                                              |
|                                                         |
|    #snd z;;                                             |
|    30 : int                                             |
|                                                         |
*---------------------------------------------------------*
```

Another standard operator of two arguments is "+"; "* + **" is the
disjoint union of types * and **, and associated with it are the
following primitives:

```
isl  : (* + **) -> bool      -- tests membership of left summand
inl  : * -> (* + **)         -- injects into left summand
inr  : * -> (** + *)         -- injects into right summand
outl : (* + **) -> *         -- projects out of left summand
outr : (* + **) -> **        -- projects out of right summand
```

These are illustrated by:

```
#let x = inl 1
#and y = inr 2;;
x = inll : (int + *)
y = inr2 : (** + int)

#isl x;;
true : bool

#isl y;;
false : bool

#outl x;;
1 : int

#outl y;;
EVALUATION FAILED outl

#outr x;;
EVALUATION FAILED outr

#outr y;;
2 : int
```

The abstract type "time" defined above can be thought of as a type operator with no arguments (i.e. a nullary operator); its primitives are "maketime", "hours" and "minutes". The "abstype...with..." construct may also be used to define non-nullary type operators (with "absrectype" in place of "abstype" if these are recursive). For example trees analogous to LISP S-expressions could be defined by:

```
#absrectype * sexp = * + (* sexp) # (* sexp)
# with cons(s1,s2) = abssexp(inr(s1,s2))
# and      car s = fst(outr(repsexp s))
# and      cdr s = snd(outr(repsexp s))
# and     atom s = isl(repsexp s)
# and  makeatom a = abssexp(inl a);;
cons = - : (((* sexp) # (* sexp)) -> (* sexp))
car = - : ((** sexp) -> (** sexp))
cdr = - : ((*** sexp) -> (*** sexp))
atom = - : ((**** sexp) -> bool)
makeatom = - : (***** -> (***** sexp))
```

Abstract types provide a very powerful modularising tool. We cannot describe their uses here but, to whet the readers appetite, point out that the object language PPLAMBDA (see Chapter 3.) is interfaced to ML via the abstract types "term", "form", "type" and "thm".

2.2 Syntax of ML.

We shall use variables to range over the various constructs of ML as follows:

```
id ranges over ML identifiers
sn    "     "    "   section names
ce    "     "    "   constant expressions
ty    "     "    "   types
db    "     "    "   defined type bindings (see 2.4.4)
ab    "     "    "   abstract type bindings (see 2.4.5)
d     "     "    "   declarations
b     "     "    "   bindings
v     "     "    "   varstructs (variable structures)
e     "     "    "   expressions
s     "     "    "   section commands
```

Identifiers, section names and constant expressions are described in 2.2.3 below, types and type-bindings are explained in 2.4 and declarations, bindings, varstructs, expressions and section commands are defined by the following BNF-like syntax equations in which:

1. Each variable ranges over constructs as above.

2. The numbers following the various variables are just to distinguish different occurrences – this will be convenient when we describe the semantics in 2.3.

3. "{C}" denotes an optional occurrence of C, and for n>1 "{C1|C2 ... |Cn}" denotes a choice of exactly one of C1,C2 ... ,Cn.

4. The constructs are listed in order of decreasing binding power.

5. "L" or "R" following a construct means that it associates to the left (L) or right (R) when juxtaposed with itself (where this is syntactically admissible).

6. Certain constructs are equivalent to others and this is indicated by "equiv." followed by the equivalent construct.

2.2.1 Syntax Equations for ML.

Declarations d

```
d ::= let b                          ordinary variables
    | letref b                       assignable variables
    | letrec b                       recursive functions

    | lettype db                     defined types

    | abstype ab                     abstract types
    | absrectype ab                  recursive abstract types
```

Bindings b

```
b ::= v=e                            simple binding

    | id v1 v2 ... vn {:ty} = e      function definition

    | b1 and b2 ... and bn           multiple binding
```

Varstructs v

```
v ::= ()                             empty varstruct

    | id                             variable

    | v:ty                           type constraint

    | v1.v2                      R    list cons

    | v1,v2                      R    pairing

    | []                             empty list
    | [v1;v2 ... ;vn]                list of n elements

    | (v)                            equiv. "v"
```

Expressions e

```
e ::= ce                                  constant

    | id                                  variable

    | e1 e2                      L        function application

    | e:ty                                type constraint

    | -e                                  unary minus
    | e1*e2                      L        multiplication
    | e1/e2                      L        division
    | e1+e2                      L        addition
    | e1-e2                      L        subtraction
    | e1<e2                               less than
    | e1>e2                               greater than

    | e1.e2                      R        list cons
    | e1@e2                      R        list append

    | e1=e2                      L        equality

    | not e                               negation
    | e1&e2                      R        conjunction
    | e1 or e2                   R        disjunction

    | e1=>e2|e3                  R        equiv. "if e1 then e2 else e3"

    | do e                                evaluate e for side effects

    | e1,e2                      R        pairing

    | v:=e                                assignment

    | fail                                equiv. "failwith `fail`"
    | failwith e                          failure with explicit token
```

```
| {if e1 {then|loop} e1'                    conditional and loop
   if e2 {then|loop} e2'
                    .
                    .
                    .
   if en {then|loop} en'}
  {{else|loop} en''}

| e {??|!!} e1 e1'                    R    failure trap and loop
    {??|!!} e2 e2'
                    .
                    .
                    .
    {??|!!} en en'
    {{?|!|?\id|!\id} en''}

| e1;e2 ... ;en                            sequencing

| []                                       empty list
| [e1;e2 ... ;en]                          list of n elements

| e where b                          R     equiv. "let b in e"
| e whereref b                       R     equiv. "letref b in e"
| e whererec b                       R     equiv. "letrec b in e"
| e wheretype db                           equiv. "lettype db in e"
| e whereabstype ab                        equiv. "abstype ab in e"
| e whereabsrectype ab                     equiv. "absrectype ab in e"

| d in e                                   local declaration

| \v1 v2 ... vn. e                         abstraction

| (e)                                      equiv. "e"
```

Section Commands s

```
s ::= begin {sn}                           begin section {sn}

    | end {sn}                             end section {sn}
```

2.2.2 Notes on the Syntax Equations for ML.

1. In the syntax equations constructs are listed in order of decreasing binding power. For example, since "el e2" is listed before "el;e2" function application binds tighter than sequencing and thus "el e2;e3" parses as "(el e2);e3". This convention only determines the relative binding power of different constructs. The left or right association of a construct is indicated explicitly by "L" for left and "R" for right. For example as application associates to the left "el e2 e3" parses as "(el e2)e3", and as "el=>e2|e3" associates to the right "el=>e2|e3=>e4|e5" parses as "el=>e2|(e3=>e4|e5)".

2. Only functions can be defined with "letrec". For example "letrec x = 2-x" would cause a syntax error.

3. All the identifiers occurring in a varstruct must be distinct.

4. Spaces, returns and tabs can be inserted and deleted arbitrarily without affecting the meaning (as long as obvious ambiguities are not introduced). For example the space in "- x" but not in "not x" can be omitted. Comments, which are arbitrary sequences of characters surrounded by "%"'s, can be inserted anywhere a space is allowed.

2.2.3 Identifiers and other lexical matters.

1. Identifiers are strings of letters, digits and primes (') which start with a letter.

2. Section names are sequences of identifiers and integers separated by periods (.). For example: "1.2.3" or "Section4.1.7".

3. The ML constant expressions (ce's) are:

   1. Integers - i.e. strings of the digits 0,1 ...,9.

   2. Truth values "true" and "false".

   3. Tokens and token-lists:

      1. Tokens consist of any sequence of characters surrounded by token quotes (`), e.g. `This is a single token`.

2. Token-lists consist of any sequence of tokens (separated by spaces, returns, line-feeds or tabs) surrounded by token-list quotes (``). e.g. ``This is a token-list containing 7 members``. ``t1 t2 ... tn`` is equivalent to [`t1`;`t2` ... ;`tn`].

In any token or token-list the occurrence of "/x" has the following meanings for different x's:

1. /0 = ten spaces.

2. /n = n spaces (0<n<10).

3. /S = one space.

4. /R = return.

5. /L = line-feed.

6. /T = tab.

7. /x = x taken literally otherwise.

Thus to include token quotes in tokens or token-list quotes in token-lists the appropriate quotes must be preceded by "/" etc.

4. Quoted PPLAMBDA constructs: these consist of an opening quotation symbol followed by a PPLAMBDA construct (i.e. term, formula or type) followed by a closing quotation symbol.

   1. For PPLAMBDA terms and formulae the opening and closing quotation symbols are the double quote ("). For example " "F X" " is a quoted term and " "!X.X==F X" " a quoted formula.

   2. For PPLAMBDA types the opening quotation symbol is a colon preceded by a double quote (":), and the closing quotation symbol is just a double quote ("). For example " ":INT" " is a quoted type.

5. The expression "()", called empty, which evaluates to the unique object of ML type ".".

4. The ML <u>prefixes</u> px and <u>infixes</u> ix are given by:

    px ::= not | - | do

    ix ::= * | / | + | - | . | @ | = | < | > | & | or | ,

In addition any identifier (and certain single characters) can be made into an infix. Such user-defined infixes bind tighter than "...=>...|..." but weaker than "or".

Except for "&" and "or", each infix ix (or prefix px) has correlated with it a special identifier $ix (or $px) which is bound to the associated function; for example the identifier "$+" is bound to the addition function, and $@ to the list-append function (see Appendix 3 for the meaning of "$"-ed infixes). This is useful for rebinding infixes (or prefixes) or for passing them as arguments; for example "let $+(x,y) = x*y" rebinds + to mean multiplication, and "f $@" applies f to the append function.

To make an identifier (or admissible single character) into an infix one applies the function "mlinfix" to the appropriate token; for example to infix "oo" one would type "mlinfix `oo`;;" to top-level ML, and then "el oo e2" and "$oo(el,e2)" would be synonymous. If the function one wants to infix is curried, then one can use "mlcinfix" instead of "mlinfix"; for example the effect of doing "mlcinfix `oo`;;" is to make "el oo e2" synonymous with "$oo el e2". More on the functions "mlinfix" and "mlcinfix" is given in Appendix 3. (It is probably better to specify the infix status of an identifier in its declaration, and for this to be local to the scope of the declaration; we leave this to a future version of the system.)

2.3 Semantics of ML.

The evaluation of all ML constructs takes place in the context of an environment. This specifies what the identifiers in use denote. Identifiers may be bound either to values or to locations. The contents of locations - which must be values - are specified in the store. If an identifier is bound to a location then (and only then) is it assignable. Thus bindings are held in the environment whereas location contents are held in the store.

The evaluation of ML constructs may either succeed or fail; in the case of success:

1. The evaluation of a declaration, d say, changes the bindings in the environment of the identifiers declared in d. If d is at top level, then the scope of the binding is everything in the current section following d. In "d in e" the scope of d is the evaluation of e, and so when this is finished the environment reverts to its original state (see 2.3.1).

2. The evaluation of an expression yields a value - the value of the expression (see 2.3.2).

3. The evaluation of a section command begins or ends a section. Sections delimit the scope of top level declarations (see 2.3.3).

If an assignment is done during an evaluation, then the store will be changed - we shall refer to these changes as side effects of the evaluation.

If the evaluation of a construct fails, then failure is signalled, and a token is passed, to the context which invoked the evaluation. This token is called the failure token, and normally it indicates the cause of the failure. During evaluations failures may be generated either implicitly by certain error conditions, or explicitly by the the construct "failwith e" (which fails with e's value as failure token). For example, the evaluation of the expression "1/0" fails implicitly with failure token `div`, whilst that of "failwith `tok`" fails explicitly with failure token `tok`. We shall say two evaluations fail similarly if they both fail with the same failure token. For example the evaluation of "1/0" and "failwith `div`" fail similarly. Side effects are not undone by failures.

If during the evaluation of a construct a failure is generated, then unless the construct is a failure trap (i.e. an expression built from "?" and/or "!") the evaluation of the construct itself fails similarly. Thus failures propagate up until trapped, or they reach top level. For example, when evaluating "(1/0)+1000": "1/0" is first evaluated, and the failure this generates causes the evaluation of the whole expression (viz. "(1/0)+1000") to fail with `div`. On the other hand, the evaluation of "(1/0)?1000" traps the failure generated by the evaluation of "1/0", and succeeds with value 1000.

(in general the evaluation of "el?e2" proceeds by first evaluating el, and if this succeeds with value E, then E is returned as the value of "el?e2"; however if el fails then the result of evaluating "el?e2" is determined by evaluating e2).

In describing evaluations, when we say that we <u>pass</u> <u>control</u> to a construct, we mean that the outcome of the evaluation is to be the outcome of evaluating the construct. For example, if when evaluating "el?e2" the evaluation of el fails, then we pass control to e2.

Expressions and varstructs can be optionally decorated with types by writing ":ty" after them (e.g."[]:int list"). The effect of this is to force the type checker to assign an instance of the asserted type to the construct; this is useful as a way of constraining types more than the type checker would otherwise do (i.e. more than context demands), and it can also serve as helpful documentation. Details of types and type checking are given in 2.4, and will be ignored in describing the evaluation of ML constructs in the rest of this section.

If we omit types, precedence information and those constructs which are equivalent to others, then the syntax of ML can be summarized by:

d ::= let b | letref b | letrec b

b ::= v=e | id v1 v2 ... vn = e | b1 and b2 ... and bn

v ::= () | id | v1.v2 | v1,v2 | [] | [v1;v2 ... ;vn]

e ::= ce | id | el e2

    | px e | el ix e2 | v:=e | failwith e

    | {if el {then|loop} el'
       if e2 {then|loop} e2'
          .
          .
          .
      if en {then|loop} en'} {{else|loop} e'}

    | e {??|!!} el el'
      {??|!!} e2 e2'
        .
        .
        .
      {??|!!} en en' {{?|!|?\id|!\id} e'}

    | el;e2 ... ;en | [] | [el;e2 ... ;en] | d in e
    | \v1 v2 ... vn. e

s ::= begin {sn} | end {sn}

2.3.1 Declarations.

Any declaration must be of one of the three kinds "let b", "letref b" or "letrec b", where b is a binding.

Each such declaration is evaluated by first evaluating the binding b to produce a (possibly empty) set of identifier-value pairs, and then extending the environment (in a manner determined by the kind of declaration) so that each identifier in this set of pairs denotes its corresponding value. The evaluation of bindings is described in 2.3.1.1 below.

1. Evaluating "let b" declares the identifiers specified in b to be ordinary (i.e. non assignable), and binds (in the environment) each one to the corresponding value produced by evaluating b.

2. Evaluating "letref b" declares the identifiers specified in b to be assignable and thus binds (in the environment) each one to a new location, whose contents (in the store) is set to the corresponding value. The effect of subsequent assignments to the identifiers will be to change the contents of the locations they are bound to. Bindings (in the environment) of identifiers to locations can only be changed by evaluating another declaration to supercede the original one.

3. Evaluating "letrec b" is similar to evaluating "let b" except that:

   1. The binding b in "letrec b" must consist only of function definitions.

   2. These functions are made mutually recursive.

   Thus the evaluation of b must produce a set of pairs $(x1,f1) \ldots (xn,fn)$ where each fi ($0<i<n+1$) is a function. The effect of "letrec b" is then to bind each fi to xi in such a way that occurrences of xj ($0<j<n+1$) are interpreted as recursive calls to fj. If the declaration had been "let b" instead of "letrec b", then an occurrence of xj would be interpreted as a call to whatever xj was bound to in the environment immediately preceding the declaration. Thus with "let b", b is evaluated in the environment holding before the declaration, whilst with "letrec b", b is evaluated in this environment extended by xi being bound to fi ($0<i<n+1$).

38

For example, consider:

1.   let f n = if n=0 then 1 else n*f(n-1)

2.   letrec f n = if n=0 then 1 else n*f(n-1)

The meaning of f defined by 1. depends on whatever f is bound to before the declaration is evaluated, whilst the meaning of f defined by 2. is independent of this (and is the factorial function).

2.3.1.1 The Evaluation of bindings.

There are three kinds of binding each of which, when evaluated, produces a set of identifier-value pairs (or fails):

1. Simple bindings which have the form "v=e" where v is a varstruct and e an expression.

2. Function definitions which have the form "id v1 ... vn = e". This is just an abbreviation for the simple binding "id = \v1 ... vn. e".

3. Multiple bindings which have the form "b1 and b2 ... and bn" where b1,b2 ... ,bn are simple bindings or function definitions. As a function definition is just an abbreviation for a certain simple binding, each bi (0<i<n+1) either is, or is an abbreviation for, some simple binding "vi=ei". The multiple binding "b1 and b2 ... and bn" then abbreviates "v1,v2 ... ,vn = e1,e2 ... en", which is a simple binding.

As function definitions and multiple bindings are abbreviations for simple bindings we need only describe the evaluation of the latter.

A simple binding "v=e" is evaluated by first evaluating e to obtain a value E (if the evaluation fails then the evaluation of "v=e" fails similarly). Next the varstruct v is matched with E to see if they have the same form (precise details in 2.3.1.2 below). If so, then to each identifier in v there is a corresponding component of E. The evaluation of "v=e" then returns the set of each identifier paired with its corresponding component. If v and E don't match then the evaluation of "v=e" fails with failure token `varstruct`.

2.3.1.2 Matching Varstructs and Expression Values.

When a varstruct v is matched with a value E, either the match succeeds and a set of identifier-value pairs is returned (each identifier in v being paired with the corresponding component of E), or the match fails. We describe, by cases on v, the conditions for v to match E and the sets of pairs returned:

----()

Always matches. The empty set of pairs is returned.

----id

Always matches. The set consisting of id paired with E is returned.

----v1.v2

E must be a non empty list E1.E2 such that v1 matches E1 and v2 matches E2. The union of the sets of pairs returned from matching v1 with E1 and v2 with E2 is returned.

----v1,v2

E must be a pair E1,E2 such that v1 matches E1 and v2 matches E2. The union of the sets of pairs returned from matching v1 with E1 and v2 with E2 is returned.

----[v1;v2 ... ;vn]

E must be a list [E1;E2 ... ;En] of length n such that for each i (where 0<i<n+1) vi matches Ei. The union of the sets of pairs returned by matching vi with Ei is produced.

Thus if v matches E, then v and E have a similar shape, and each identifier in v corresponds to some component of E (namely that component paired with the identifier in the set returned by the match).

Here are some examples:

1. "[x;y;z]" matches "[1;2;3]" with x,y and z corresponding to 1,2 and 3 respectively.

2. "[x;y;z]" doesn't match "[1;2]" or "[1;2;3;4]".

3. "x.y" matches "[1;2;3]" with x and y corresponding to 1 and [2;3] respectively (E1.[E2;E3 ... ;En] = [E1;E2;E3 ... ;En])

4. "x.y" doesn't match "1" or "[]".

5. "x,y" matches "1,2" with x and y corresponding to 1 and 2 respectively.

6. "x,y" doesn't match "[1;2]".

7. "(x,y),[(z.w);()]" matches "(1,2),[[3;4;5];[6;7]]" with x,y,z
   and w corresponding to 1,2,3 and [4;5] respectively.

2.3.2 Expressions

If the evaluation of an expression terminates, then either it
succeeds with some value, or it fails; in either case assignments
performed during the evaluation may cause side effects. If the
evaluation succeeds with some value we shall say that value is
returned.

We shall describe the evaluation of expressions by considering the
various cases, in the order in which they are listed in the syntax
equations.

----ce

The appropriate constant value is returned.

----id

The value associated with id is returned. If id is ordinary, then
the value returned is the value bound to id in the environment.
If id is assignable, then the value returned is the contents of
the location to which id is bound.

----e1 e2

e1 and e2 are evaluated in that order. The result of applying the
value of e1 (which must be a function) to that of e2 is returned.

----px e

e is evaluated and then the result of applying px to the value of
e is returned.

"-e" and "not e" have the obvious meanings; "do e" evaluates e
for its side effects and then returns empty.

----e1 ix e2

"e1&e2" is equivalent to "if e1 then e2 else false" (so sometimes
only e1 need be evaluated to evaluate "e1&e2")

"el or e2" is equivalent to "if el then true else e2" (so sometimes only el needs to be evaluated to evaluate "el or e2")

Except when ix is "&" or "or", el and e2 are evaluated in that order, and the result of applying ix to their two values returned.

"el,e2" returns the pair with first component the value of el, and second component the value of e2; the meaning of the other infixes are given in Appendix 3.

----v:=e

Every identifier in v must be assignable and bound to some location in the environment. The effect of the assignment is to update the contents of these locations (in the store) with the values corresponding to the identifiers produced by evaluating the binding "v=e" (see 2.3.1.1). If the evaluation of e fails, then no updating of locations occurs, and the assignment fails similarly. If the matching to v fails, then the assignment fails with `varstruct`. The value of "v:=e" is the value of e.

----failwith e

e is evaluated and then a failure with e's value (which must be a token) is generated.

----{if el {then|loop} el'
    if e2 {then|loop} e2'
              .
              .
              .
    if en {then|loop} en'} {{else|loop} e'}

el,e2, ... ,en are evaluated in turn until one of them, em say, returns true (each ei (for $0<i<n+1$) must return either true or false). When the phrase following em is "then em'" control is passed to em'; however when the phrase is "loop em'", then em' is evaluated for its side effects, and then control is passed back to the beginning of the whole expression again (i.e. to the beginning of "if el ... ").

In the case that all of el,e2 ... ,en return false, and there is a phrase following en', then if this is "else e'" control is passed to e', whilst if it is "loop e'" then e' is evaluated for its side effects and control is then passed back to the beginning of the whole expression again.

In the case that all of el,...,en return false, but no phrase follows en' - i.e. the option "{{else|loop} e'}" is absent - then empty (the unique value of type ".") is returned.

```
----e {??|!!} e1 e1'
     {??|!!} e2 e2'
        .
        .
        .
     {??|!!} en en' {{?|!|?\id|!\id} e'}
```

e is evaluated and if this succeeds its value is returned.

In the case that e fails, with failure token tok say, then each of e1,e2 ... ,en are evaluated in turn until one of them, em say, returns a token list containing tok (each ei (for 0<i<n+1) must return a token list). If "??" immediately precedes em, then control is passed to em'; however if "!!" precedes it, then em' is evaluated and control is passed back to the beginning of the whole expression (i.e. to the beginning of "e {??|!!} ... ").

If none of e1,e2 ... ,en returns a token list containing tok, and nothing follows en' (i.e. the option "{{ ... } e'}" is absent), then the whole expressions fails with tok (i.e. fails similarly to e).

If none of e1,e2 ... ,en produces a token list containing tok, and "? e'" follows en', then control is passed to e'. But if "! e'" follows en', then e' is evaluated, and control is passed back to the beginning of the whole expression.

If "?\id e'" or "!\id e'" follows en', then e' is evaluated in an environment in which id is bound to the failure token tok (i.e. an evaluation equivalent to doing "let id=tok in e'" is done), and then depending on whether it was "?\" or "!\" that occurred, the value of e' is returned or control is passed back to the beginning of the whole expression respectively.

----e1;e2 ... ;en

e1,e2 ... ,en are evaluated in that order, and the value of en is returned.

----[e1;e2 ... ;en]

e1,e2, ... ,en are evaluated in that order and the list of their values returned. [] evaluates to the null list.

----d in e

d is evaluated, and then e is evaluated in the extended environment and its value returned. The declaration d is local to e, so that after the evaluation of e, the former environment is restored.

----\v1 v2 ... vn. e

The evaluation of \-expressions always succeeds and yields a
function value. The environment in which the evaluation occurs
(i.e. in which the function value is created) is called the
definition environment.

1. Simple \-expressions: \v. e

"\v . e" evaluates to that function which when applied to some
argument yields the result of evaluating e in the current
(i.e. application time) store, and in the environment obtained
from the definition environment by binding any identifiers in
v to the corresponding components of the argument (see
2.3.1.1).

2. Compound \-expressions: \v1 v2 ... vn. e

A \-expression with more than one parameter is curried i.e.
"\v1 v2 ... vn. e"   is   exactly   equivalent   to
"\v1.(\v2 ... .\vn. e) ... " whose meaning is given by 1.
above.

Thus the free identifiers in a function keep the same binding they
had in the definition environment. So if a free identifier is
non-assignable in that environment, then its value is fixed to the
value it has there. On the other hand, if a free identifier is
assignable in the definition environment, then it will be bound to
a location;   although that binding is fixed, the contents of the
location in the store is not, and can be subsequently changed with
assignments.

2.3.3 Section commands.

Sections delimit the scope of top level declarations and so provide
a form of interactive block structure. They may only be begun or
ended at top level. Storage used within a section will be reclaimed
(by the garbage collector) when the section is ended.

---- begin {sn}

A new section is begun. The current environment and type
definitions (both defined and abstract types) are saved so they
can be restored when the section is ended. The new section is
named sn if sn is present, otherwise it is nameless.

----end {sn}

The most recently begun section with name sn is ended. If no name
is mentioned (i.e. "end;;<return>"), then the most recently opened
section (named or nameless) is ended. The effect of ending a

section is to restore the environment and type definitions saved when the section was begun. The value of the ML identifier "it" is unchanged and provides the only way of exporting values out of sections. If the value of "it" has a type local to a section, then ending the section will cause a failure with token `end` (thus values with local types can't be exported).

2.4 ML Types.

So far we have made little mention of types. For ML in its role as a metalanguage for proof, the motivation for strict typechecking is principally to ensure that every computed value of type thm is indeed a theorem, i.e. belongs to the closure of the axioms under the inference rules. This could well have been achieved by run-time typechecking, but we have chosen to adopt compile-time typechecking instead; this is partly for the considerable debugging aid that it provides, partly for efficient execution, and partly to explore the possibility of combining polymorphism with typechecking. This latter is of general interest in programming languages and has nothing to do specifically with proof; the problem is that there are many operations (list mapping functions, functional composition, etc.) which work at an infinity of types, and therefore their types should be somehow parameterized - but it is rather inconvenient to have to mention the particular type intended at each of their uses.

The system is implemented in such a way that, although the user may occasionally (either for documentation or as a constraint) ascribe a type to an ML expression or varstruct, it is hardly ever necessary to do so. He will almost always be content with the types ascribed and presented to him by the typechecker, which checks every top-level phrase before it is evaluated. (The typechecker may sometimes find a more general type assignment than expected.)

2.4.1 Types and Objects.

Every data object in ML possesses a type. (ML types - or metatypes as we shall call them - must not be confused with the types of PPLAMBDA discussed in Chapter 3, especially since some of these metatypes - namely term, form, thm and type itself - pertain to the syntax of PPLAMBDA.) Such an object may possess many types and then it is said to be polymorphic; in this case it possesses a polytype - i.e. a type containing type variables (for which we use a sequence of asterisks possibly followed by an identifier or integer) - and moreover it possesses all types which are instances of its polytype, gained by substituting types for zero or more type variables in the polytype. A type containing no type variables is a monotype.

We saw several examples of types in Section 2.1. To understand the following syntax, note that list is a postfixed unary (one-argument) type operator; it is an example of an abstract type operator, and the user may introduce these for himself. For example, he may introduce the binary operator directory; then the following will be types of different kinds of directory:

        (token, int)directory
        (int, int->int)directory

He may even deal with lists of directories, with the type

```
                (int, bool)directory list
```

The syntax of types is:

```
    ty   ::=   sty                          Standard (non-infix) type
             | ty # ty                  R   Cartesian product
             | ty + ty                  R   Disjoint sum
             | ty -> ty                 R   Function type


    sty ::=    . | int | bool | token        Basic types
             | term | form | type | thm      Basic types for PPLAMBDA
             | vty                            Type variable
             | id                             Defined type (2.4.4)
             | id                             Nullary abstract type
             | tyarg id                  L    Abstract type (2.4.5)
             | (ty)


    tyarg ::= sty                        Single type argument
            | (ty, .. ,ty)               One or more type arguments


    vty ::=    * | ** | ..
             | *id | **id | ..
             | *0 | **0 | .. | *1 | **1 | ..
```

Defined types are introduced by a "lettype" declaration (see 2.4.4 below) which allows an identifier to abbreviate an arbitrary monotype. By contrast, an abstract type consists of an identifier (a type operator introduced by an "abstype" or "absrectype" declaration; see 2.4.5 below) postfixed to zero or more type arguments; two or more arguments must be separated by commas and enclosed by parentheses. list is a predeclared unary abstract type operator, and #, + and -> may be regarded as infix forms of three predeclared binary abstract type operators.

What is meant by an object possessing a type? (We shall talk of objects possessing types and phrases having types, to emphasize the distinction).

For basic types, all integers possess int, both booleans possess bool, all tokens possess token, etc. The only object possessing . is that denoted by () in ML.

For a defined type id, an object possesses id (during execution of phrases in the scope of the declaration of id) iff it possesses the type which id abbreviates.

For compound monotypes,

(1) the type ty list is possessed by any list of objects all possessing type ty (so that the empty list possesses type ty list for every ty),

(2) the type ty1#ty2 is possessed by any pair of objects possessing the types ty1 , ty2 respectively,

(3) the type ty1+ty2 is possessed by the left-injection of any object possessing ty1, and by the right-injection of any object possessing ty2. These injections are denoted by the ML function identifiers inl: *->*+** and inr: **->*+** (see Appendix 3),

(4) a function possesses type ty1->ty2 if whenever its argument possesses type ty1, its result (if defined) possesses type ty2. (This is not an exact description; for example, an ML-defined function with non-local variables may possess this type even though some assumption about the types of the values of these non-local variables is necessary for the above condition to hold. The constraints on programs listed below ensure that the non-locals will always have the right types).

(5) an object possesses the abstract type tyarg id iff it is represented (via the abstract type representation) by an object possessing the tyarg instance of the right-hand side of the declaration of id.

Finally, an object possesses a polytype ty iff it possesses all monotypes which are substitution instances of ty.

2.4.2 Typing of ML phrases.

We now explain the constraints used by the typechecker in ascribing types to ML expressions, varstructs and declarations.

The significance of expression e having type ty is that the value of e (if evaluation terminates successfully) possesses type ty. As consequences of the well-typing constraints listed below, it is impossible for example to apply a non-function to an argument, or to form a list of objects of different types, or (as mentioned earlier) to compute an object of type thm which is not a theorem.

The type ascribed to a phrase depends in general on the entire surrounding ML program. However, in the case of top-level expressions and declarations, the type ascribed depends only on preceding top-level phrases. Thus you know that types ascribed at top-level are not subject to further constraint.

Before each top-level phrase is executed, types are ascribed to all its sub-expressions, -declarations and -varstructs according to the following rules. Most of the rules are rather natural; those which are less so are discussed subsequently. You are only presented with the types of top-level phrases; the types of sub-phrases will hardly ever concern you.

Before giving the list of constraints, let us discuss an example which illustrates some important points. To map a function over a list we may define the polymorphic function "map" recursively as follows (where we have used an explicit abstraction, rather than "letrec map f l = ...", to make the typing clearer):

letrec map = \f.\l. null l => [] | f(hd l).map f(tl l) ;;

From this declaration the typechecker will infer a <u>generic</u> type for map; by "generic" we mean that each later occurrence of map will be ascribed a type which is a substitution instance of the generic type.

Now the free identifiers in this declaration are null, hd and $., which are ML primitives whose <u>generic</u> (poly)types are * list -> bool, * list -> * and * # * list -> * list; the first constraint used by the typechecker is that the occurrences of these identifiers in the declaration are ascribed instances of their generic types. Other constraints which the typechecker will use to determine the type of map are:

All occurrences of a \-bound variable receive the same type.

Each arm of a conditional receives the same type, and the condition receives type bool.

In each application e = (el e2), if e2 receives ty and e receives ty' then el receives ty->ty'.

In each abstraction e = \v.el, if v receives ty and el receives ty' then e receives ty->ty'.

In a letrec declaration, all free occurrences of the declared variable receives the same type.

Now the typechecker will ascribe the type (*->**)->* list->** list to map. This is in fact the most general type consistent with the constraints mentioned. Moreover, it can be shown that any instance of this type also allows the constraints to be satisfied; this is what allows us to claim that the declaration is indeed polymorphic.

In the following constraint list, we say "p has ty" to indicate that the phrase p is ascribed a type ty which satisfies the stated conditions. We use x, v, e, d to stand for variables, varstructs, expressions and declarations respectively.

(1) Constants

    (i)   () has .

    (ii)   0 has int, 1 has int, ...

(iii)   true has bool, false has bool

(iv)   `...` has token, ``...`` has token list

(v)   "..." has term, or

(vi)   "..." has form, depending on the structure of ...

(vii)   ":..." has type

(2) Identifiers

The constraints described here are discussed in 2.4.3 below.

(i)   If x is bound by \ or letref, then x is ascribed the same type as its binding occurrence. In the case of letref, this must be monotype if (a) the letref is top-level or (b) an assignment to x occurs within a \-expression within its scope.

(ii)   If x is bound by let or letrec, then x has ty, where ty is an instance of the type of the binding occurrence of x (i.e. the generic type of x), in which type variables occurring in the types of current \-bound or letref-bound identifiers are not instantiated.

(iii) If x is not bound in the program (in which case it must be an ML primitive), then x has ty, where ty is an instance of the type given in Appendix 3.

(3) Varstructs

Cases for a varstruct v:

----()
        v has ty, where ty is any type.

----v1:ty
        v1 and v have an instance of ty.

----v1,v2
        If v1 has ty1 and v2 has ty2, then v has ty1#ty2.

----v1.v2
        If v1 has ty then v2 and v have ty list.

----[v1; ... ;vn]
        For some ty, each vi has ty and v has ty list.

(4) Expressions

Cases for an expression e (not a constant or identifier) :

----e1 e2
   If e2 has ty and e has ty' then e1 has ty->ty'.

----e1:ty
   e1 and e have an instance of ty.

----px e1
   Treated as $px(e1) when px is a prefix. If e is -e1, then e and
   e1 have int.

----e1 ix e2
   Treated as $ix(e1,e2) if ix is an infix (including   those
   introduced by mlinfix), and as ($ix e1 e2) if ix is a "curried"
   infix (introduced by mlcinfix). If e is (e1 & e2)   or   (e1 or e2),
   then e, e1 and e2 have bool.

----e1,e2
   If e1 has ty1 and e2 has ty2 then e has ty1#ty2.

----v:=e1
   For some ty, v, e1 and e all have ty.

----failwith e1
   e1 has tok, and e has any type.

----if e1 then e1' ... if en then en' else e'
   Each ei (0<i<n+1) has bool, and - for some ty - e, each ei' and e'
   all have ty.   However, this constraint does not apply to an ei'
   preceded by loop in place of then, nor to e' preceded by loop in
   place of else. If e' is absent, then ty = . .

----e0' ??e1 e1' ... ??en en' ?{\x} e'
   Each ei (0<i<n+1) has token list, and - for some ty - e, e0', each
   ei' and e' all have ty. However, this constraint does not apply
   to an ei' preceded by !! in place of ?? nor to e' preceded by ! in
   place of ?. If \x is present, x has tok.

----e1; ... ;en
   If en has ty then e has ty.

----[e1; ... ;en]
   For some ty, each ei has ty and e has ty list.

----d in e1
   If e1 has ty then e has ty. See also (2) above.   If d is an
   abstract type definition (see 2.4.5) then ty must contain no
   abstract type defined in d.

```
----\v.el
```
If v has ty and el has ty' then e has ty->ty'. See also (2) above.

(5) Declarations

   (i)   Each binding of the form x v1...vn = e   is treated as
   x = \v1. ...\vn. e

   (ii)   let v1 = el and...and vn = en   is   treated   as
   let v1,..., vn = el,..., en (similarly for letrec, letref)

   (iii) If d is let v = e , then - for some ty - d, v and e all
   have ty (similarly for letref). Note that e is not in the scope of
   the declaration.

   (iv)   If d is letrec x1, ... ,xn = el, ... ,en , then - for some
   tyi - xi and ei have tyi, and d has ty1#...#tyn. (In addition,
   each free occurrence of xi in el, ... ,en has tyi, so that the
   type of recursive calls of xi is the same as the declaring type)

2.4.3 Discussion of Type Constraints.

   We give here reasons for our constraints on the types ascribed to
occurrences of identifiers. The reader may like to skip this
subsection at first reading.

   (1) Consider constraint (2i) for \-bound identifiers. It implies
that the expression let x=e in e' may be well-typed even if the
semantically equivalent (\x.e')e is not, since in the former
expression x may occur in e' with two incompatible types which are
both instances of the declaring type. The greater constraint on
(\x.e') is associated with the fact that the function so created may
be applied to many different arguments during evaluation. To show the
need for the constraint, suppose that it is replaced by the weaker
constraint for let-bound identifiers, so that for example

   let f = \x. if x then 1+x else x(1)

is a well-typed declaration of type *->int, in which the four
occurrences of x receive types *, bool, int, int->int respectively.
In the absence of an explicit argument for the abstraction, no
constraint exists for the type of the binding occurrence of x. But,
because f is let-bound, expressions such as f(true)   and   f(`dog`)
are admissible in the scope of f, although their evaluation should
result in either nonsense or run-time type-errors; one of our
purposes is to preclude these.

(2)   The analogous restriction for letref-bound identifiers is also due to the possibility that the identifier-value binding may change during evaluation (this time because of assignments). Consider the following:

```
letref x = [] in
  (if e then do(x:=1.x) else do(x:= [true]) ;
  hd x) ;;
```

If letref were treated like let, this phrase would be well-typed and indeed have type * , despite the fact that the value returned is either 1 or true. So - calling the whole expression e - all manner of larger expressions involving e would be well-typed, even including e(e) !

(3)   Top-level letrefs must be monomorphic (see (2ia)) to avoid retrospective type constraints at top level. If this restriction were removed the following would be allowed:

```
letref x = [] ;;
   . . .
   . . .
   2.x ;;
```

But on typechecking the last phrase, it would appear that the type of x at declaration should have been int list , not * list , and the types of intervening phrases may likewise need constraining.

(4)   To see the need for the exclusion of polymorphic non-local assignments (see (2ib)), consider this example (due to Lockwood Morris):

```
let store, fetch =
  letref x = [] in
    (\y. x:=[y] ) , (\(). hd x ) ;;
store "TT == FF" ;;
let eureka :thm = fetch() ;;
```

Now suppose we lift our constraint. Then in the declaration, x has type * list throughout its (textual) scope, and store, fetch receive types *->* list , **->* respectively. In the two ensuing phrases they get respective types form->form list, .->thm (instances of their declaring types), and the value of eureka is a contradictory formula masquerading as a theorem!

The problem is that the typechecker has no simple way of discovering the types of all values assigned to the polymorphic x, since these assignments may be invoked by calls of the function store outside the (textual) scope of x. This is not possible under our constraint.

However, polymorphic assignable identifiers are still useful: consider

```
let rev l =
    letref l,l' = l,[] in
        if null l then l' loop (l,l':= tl l, hd l.l') ;;
```

Such uses of assignable identifiers for iteration may be avoided given a suitable syntax for iteration, but assignable identifiers are useful for a totally different purpose - namely as "own variables" shared between one or more functions (as in the store-fetch example). Our constraint of course requires them to be monomorphic; this is one of the few cases where the user occasionally needs to add an explicit type to his program.

2.4.4 Defined types.

   The syntax of defined type bindings db is

   db ::= id1 = ty1 and ... and idn = tyn

Then the declaration

   lettype db

in which each tyi must be a monotype, built from basic types and previously defined types, allows you to introduce new names idi for the types tyi. Within the scope of the declaration the expression e:idi behaves exactly like e:tyi, and the type tyi will always be printed as idi.

   One aspect of such defined types should be emphasized. Suppose you declare

   lettype rat = int # int ;;

for the rational numbers, and set up the standard operations on rationals. Within the scope of this declaration any expression of type int#int will be treated as though it had type rat, and this could be not only confusing but also incorrect (in which case it ought to cause a type failure). If you wish to introduce the type rat, isomorphic to int#int but not matching it for typechecking purposes, then you should use abstract types, which we now discuss.

2.4.5 Abstract types.

   Abstract type operators may be introduced by a special kind of declaration, in which type variables are used as dummy arguments (or formal parameters) of the operators, just as ordinary variables are so used in declaring functions. We need the syntax

```
vtyarg  ::=                           Empty dummy argument list
        | vty                         One dummy argument
        | (vty, .. ,vty)              One or more dummy arguments
```

Then the syntax of abstract type bindings ab is

    ab ::= vtyarg1 id1 = ty1 and ... and vtyargn idn = tyn
           with b

where each vtyargi must contain no type variable more than once, and all the type variables in tyi must occur in vtyargi. An abstract type declaration takes the form

    {abstype|absrectype} ab

The declaration introduces a set of type operators, and also incorporates a normal binding b (treated like "let") of ML identifiers. Throughout the scope of the abstract type declaration the type operators and ML identifiers are both available, but it is only within b that the <u>representation</u> of the type operators (as declared in terms of other operators) is available.

Consider first a non-recursive abstract type declaration

    abstype vtyarg1 id1 = ty1 and ... and vtyargn idn = tyn
            with b

The sense in which the representation of each idi is available only within b is as follows: the isomorphism between objects of types tyi and vtyargi idi is available (only in b) via a pair of implicitly declared polymorphic functions

    absidi : tyi -> vtyargi idi
    repidi : vtyargi idi -> tyi

which are to be used as coercions between the abstract types and their representations. Thus in the simple case

    abstype a = ty with x = e' in e

the scope of a is e' and e, the scope of absa and repa is e', and the scope of x is e.

As a first illustration, consider the definition of the type rat of rational numbers, represented by pairs of integers, together with operations plus and times and the conversion functions

    inttorat : int->rat , rattoint : rat->int

Since rat is a nullary type operation, no type variables are involved.

```
abstype rat = int#int
  with plus(x,y) = (absrat(xl*y2+x2*yl, x2*y2)
      where xl,x2 = reprat x and yl,y2 = reprat y)
  and times(x,y) = (absrat(xl*yl, x2*y2)
      where xl,x2 = reprat x and yl,y2 = reprat y)
  and inttorat n = absrat(n,1)
  and rattoint x = ((xl/x2)*x2=xl => xl/x2 | failwith `rattoint`
      where xl,x2 = reprat x) ;;
```

A recursive abstract type declaration, i.e. one in which the type operations are defined (mutually) recursively, uses the word "absrectype" in place of "abstype".

We illustrate this, together with the use of type variables as dummy arguments, by defining the type of binary trees whose tips are values of some arbitrary type, and whose non-tip nodes are labelled by values of some (other) arbitrary type.

```
absrectype (*,**)tree = * + ** # (*,**)tree # (*,**)tree
  with tiptree x = abstree(inl x)
  and comptree(y,tl,t2) = abstree(inr(y,tl,t2))
  and istip t = isl(reptree t)
  and tipof t = outl(reptree t) ? failwith `tipof`
  and labelof t = fst(outr(reptree t)) ? failwith `labelof`
  and sonsof t = snd(outr(reptree t)) ? failwith `sonsof` ;;
```

As another example, the type operator "list" could have been defined in ML, though with a slight loss of efficiency; the reader may like to complete the following declaration:

```
absrectype * list = . + * # * list
  with $.(x,l) = ... and hd l = ... and tl l = ...
  and null l = ... and nil = abslist(inl()) ;;
```

The use of functional types in abstract type declarations admits many interesting possibilities. Consider for example a kind of process which takes an argument (of one type) and delivers a result (of another type) together with a new process. We may write

```
absrectype (*,**)process = * -> ** # (*,**)process
  with ...
```

This kind of process is a generalization of the concept of stream introduced by Landin.

Most abstract type declarations will probably be used at top-level,
so that their scope is the remainder of the (current section of)
top-level program. But for non-top-level declarations (or in
sections) a simple constraint ensures that a value of abstract type
cannot exist except during the execution of phrases within the scope
of the type declaration. In the expression

abs{rec}type ... vtyargi idi = tyi ... with b in e

the type of e, and the types of any non-local assignments within b and
e, must not involve any of the idi.

Finally, in keeping with the abstract nature of objects of abstract
type, the value of a top-level expression of abstract type is printed
as "-" (as are functional values); if you wish to "see" such an object
you should declare a conversion function in the "with" part of the
type declaration, which yields a suitable concrete representation of
the abstract objects.

2.5 Goal-directed programming.

We have now completed our description of ML, and the present section is in one sense a bridge between ML and PPLAMBDA. We develop here the metatheoretic notions of goal and tactic, mentioned in 1.1 in the context of a proof example. But in another sense this section is independent of PPLAMBDA since, as we show, the notions have broader significance; they employ a type discipline and functional programming to provide a conceptual framework for problem-solving in general. Not only do they illustrate ML programming; they also motivated its design.

2.5.1 Tactics and validity.

Recall the type definitions for our proof example in 1.1:

```
goal = form # bool
tactic = goal -> (goal list # validation)
validation = thm list -> thm
```

This particular choice of the type goal was prompted by our problem. But we now wish to suppose that goals are an unspecified class of objects whose achievement may be desired (think of them also as task specifications). This leads us to consider, in place of theorems, an unspecified class of objects which may achieve goals; let us call this second class events, and take goal and event to be unspecified ML types.

To make sense of the notion of tactic, we further postulate a binary relation of achievement between events and goals. Many problem-solving situations can be understood as instances of these three notions: goal, event and achievement. Further, we make the general type definitions

```
tactic = goal -> (goal list # validation)
validation = event list -> event
```

and now the validity of tactics (which we promised in 1.1 to make precise) can be defined. We say that a tactic T is valid if, whenever

$$T(g) = [g1;...;gn] , v$$

for a goal g, then for any events e1,...,en which achieve g1,...,gn respectively, the event v[e1;...;en] achieves g.

Validity is clearly a necessary condition for a tactic to be useful; indeed we may deny that invalid tactics are tactics at all. But it is hard to see how to design a programming language so that all definable objects of type tactic are valid, or how to gain this effect by a type discipline. At most we can adopt a style which encourages the programming of valid tactics; this can be done with tacticals, as we see later.

A simple but important consequence of our definition is that, whenever

$$T(g) = [] , v$$

for a valid T, v[] achieves g.

At this point the reader may like to satisfy himself that the simple tactics given in 1.1 are valid, for the achievement relation which pertained there.

Even a valid tactic, however, may be useless. Suppose that for every goal g, T produces a non-empty list g1,...,gn of subgoals of which at least one is unachievable. Then T is vacuously valid!

2.5.2 Strong validity and tacticals.

Let us give a simple example of the wider applicability of our notions, which will illustrate validity and also a stronger property of tactics which we call strong validity. Consider the task of resolving an integer (assumed non-negative) into prime factors. If we take goals to be integers and events to be integer lists, then an event [m1;...;mk] achieves a goal n iff each mi is prime and n = m1*...*mk. In passing note that the goals 0 and 1 are unachievable. Suppose that the function factor :int->int produces a factor m (1<m<n) of its argument n, but fails if there is none or if n=0. Then a simple tactic to reduce a goal to two smaller subgoals is

```
*-----------------------------------------------------------*
|                                                           |
|    #let RESOLVETACTIC (n) = ( [m; n/m] , \[e1;e2].e1@e2 )  |
|    #                         where m = factor(n) ;;        |
|                                                           |
*-----------------------------------------------------------*
```

Notice that the validation just concatenates two lists of integers; this clearly takes achievements of the two subgoals to an achievement of the goal, so our tactic is indeed valid. It also has a stronger property, which we call strong validity. We say that a tactic T is strongly valid if it is valid, and whenever g is achievable and

$$T(g) = [g1;...;gn] , v$$

then g1,...,gn are also achievable.

RESOLVETACTIC is strongly valid because it fails exactly when factor fails, so its subgoals are always greater than one, hence achievable. If we alter the function factor to allow it to give a factor in the range 0<m<n rather than 1<m<n, RESOLVETACTIC remains valid but is no longer strongly valid, as you may easily check. This agrees with our intuition that the altered RESOLVETACTIC is not fully satisfactory. Indeed we should work with strongly valid tactics whenever we can, but in the context of theorem-proving this is not always possible (e.g. heuristic methods may sometimes yield

unachievable subgoals, but are still useful when we can find no strongly valid tactic).

To complete a strategy for prime factorisation we need only define the (strongly valid) tactic

```
*---------------------------------------------------------------*
|                                                               |
|    #let PRIMETACTIC (n) = if prime(n) then ( [] , \[].[n] )    |
|    #                                      else fail ;;         |
|                                                               |
*---------------------------------------------------------------*
```

and now a complete strategy for prime factorisation, using the tacticals introduced in 1.1, is

```
*---------------------------------------------------------------*
|                                                               |
|    #let PRIMESTRATEGY =                                        |
|    #         REPEAT(RESOLVETACTIC ORELSE PRIMETACTIC) ;;       |
|                                                               |
*---------------------------------------------------------------*
```

Two other tacticals are of very general use. The first is the binary infixed tactical THEN ; (T1 THEN T2) will apply T2 to all subgoals produced from T1, and concatenate the resulting goal lists (its validation is in some sense the composition of validations produced by both T1 and T2). You may check that the above strategy can also be defined by

```
*---------------------------------------------------------------*
|                                                               |
|    #let PRIMESTRATEGY =                                        |
|    #         (REPEAT RESOLVETACTIC) THEN PRIMETACTIC ;;        |
|                                                               |
*---------------------------------------------------------------*
```

(to be precise, this version fails on the unachievable goals 0 and 1, while the previous version acts as IDTAC on these goals!).

The second new tactical is a nullary one, the identity tactic:

```
*---------------------------------------------------------------*
|                                                               |
|    #let IDTAC (g) = ( [g] , \[e].e ) ;;                        |
|                                                               |
*---------------------------------------------------------------*
```

Its use is in defining composite tactics and tacticals - indeed, REPEAT can be defined by

```
*------------------------------------------------------------*
|                                                            |
|     #letrec REPEAT(T)(g) =                                 |
|     #            ((T THEN REPEAT(T)) ORELSE IDTAC)(g) ;;   |
|                                                            |
*------------------------------------------------------------*
```

These four tacticals have the vital property that they preserve both
validity and strong validity. So it is a robust programming style to
use them in building strategies from simple tactics, whose validity or
strong validity is hopefully evident.

2.5.3 Goals and events in LCF.

We have seen more than one choice for the types goal, event and
tactic. The tacticals are polymorphic and apply to any choice.

In LCF proofs, the nature of PPLAMBDA suggests yet another goal
type, though we still use event = thm as in the Introduction. We
explain this choice here independently of Chapter 3.

A theorem of PPLAMBDA has the shape

    A]- f

where f is a formula (the conclusion) and A is a list of formulae (the
hypotheses). The natural deduction style is to assume the hypotheses
and work towards the conclusion. In goal-directed proof therefore, it
is natural that a goal should specify not only a formula to be proved,
but also a list of formulae which may be assumed in the proof.

Further, much work in proof is done by using rewriting rules - that
is, theorems of the form

    A]- t==u

- to simplify terms and formulae (replacing instances of the left side
t by corresponding instances of the right side u). We call a set of
such rules a simplification set, or simpset. Since different simpsets
are relevant for different goals, it is useful to include a simpset
with a goal. Hence we arrive at the type

    goal = form # simpset # form list

and our achievement relation is as follows. A goal (f,ss,A) is
achieved by a theorem A']- f' if, up to renaming of bound
variables, (i) f' is identical with f, and (ii) each member of A' is
either in A or in the hypothesis list of a member of ss.

This choice of goal allows us to invert inference rules of PPLAMBDA to form simple valid (and usually strongly valid) tactics; it also admits tactics which vary the simpset (e.g. by including an equational member of the assumption list of a goal). Some standard tactics over these goals appears in Appendix 9, and an example of their use in Section 3.1.

For this type of goal, we have adopted the name _proof_ in place of _validation_ for the type thm list -> thm of validations.

3.1 Examples of Inference.

We will demonstrate how to use the system to prove some simple theorems. You may like to refer forward briefly to section 3.2, which describes PPLAMBDA in detail, but we hope that the examples are readily intelligible.

We choose three examples. The first illustrates the induction rule and uses forward (not goal-directed) proof, the second illustrates how tactics may be used separately or compounded in goal-directed proof, and the third illustrates proof by contradiction. We rely on Appendix 5 to define the precise effect of each primitive inference rule, and on Appendix 9 to give the basic tactics and tacticals available.

3.1.1 Least fixed point theorem.

Suppose we wish to draft a theory called FIX which will contain useful fixed point theorems, and to prove (as the first fact of the theory) that

]- "!FUN. !G. FUN(G)==G IMP FIX(FUN)<<G"

which states that for any functional FUN , FIX(FUN) is its least fixed point. The following session will achieve this. We enter the system, and reply <return> to the prompt "THEORY?" since we do not wish to work in an existing theory; we then reply FIX<return> to the prompt "DRAFT?" to name our draft theory.

```
*-----------------------------------------------------------*
|                                                           |
|    THEORY?                                                |
|    DRAFT?FIX                                              |
|    (START NEW DRAFT)                                      |
|                                                           |
*-----------------------------------------------------------*
```

Now we are in ML. The next step in drafting a theory is normally to introduce types, constants and axioms, but since none are needed for our proposed theorem we proceed directly to its proof. Let us first show our proof as a tree, in the style of natural deduction. In the diagram below, each horizontal line stands for the application of an inference rule named beside it (and described in Appendix 5). Assumptions are introduced by the rule ASSUME, and a dotted box encloses all steps dependent upon the assumption, down to the inference which discharges it.

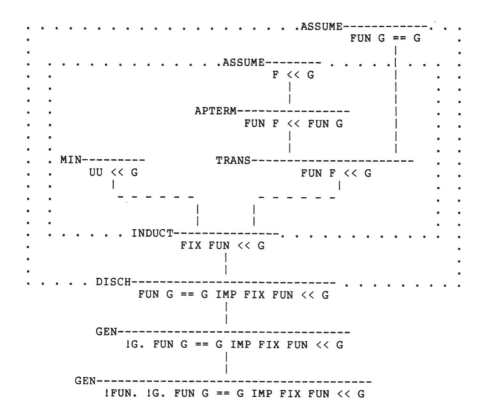

```
. . . . . . . . . . . . . . . . . . .ASSUME------------. . . .
.                                        FUN G == G        .
.                                              |           .
.    . . . . . . . . . . . . .ASSUME-------- . . . . .|  . . . .
.    .                          F << G               |      .
.    .                            |                  |      .
.    .                  APTERM---------------        |      .
.    .                    FUN F << FUN G             |      .
.    .                            |                  |      .
.    .                            |                  |      .
.    . MIN---------            TRANS----------------------  .
.    .   UU << G                    FUN F << G              .
.    .     |                           |                    .
.    .     - - - - -          - - - - -                     .
.    .              |          |                            .
.    . . . . . . . INDUCT---------------.  . . . . . . . . . .
.                   FIX FUN << G                            .
.                        |                                  .
.                        |                                  .
. . . . . DISCH------------------------------ . . . . . . . . .
           FUN G == G IMP FIX FUN << G
                        |
                        |
        GEN------------------------------------
          !G. FUN G == G IMP FIX FUN << G
                        |
                        |
     GEN------------------------------------------
       !FUN. !G. FUN G == G IMP FIX FUN << G
```

We now continue our session, which the reader should compare with
the proof tree.   We first assume the antecedent of our proposed
theorem:

```
*-----------------------------------------------------------*
|                                                           |
|    #let a1 = ASSUME "FUN G == G:*" ;;                      |
|    a1 = .]- "FUN G == G" :thm                              |
|                                                           |
*-----------------------------------------------------------*
```

We explicitly ascribe a variable type "*" to G, since we are proving a
polymorphic theorem.   The types of FUN and all later terms are
inferred by the system, as explained in section 3.2.   The result of
ASSUME is a tautology - in fact a theorem whose hypothesis part
consists of a list with one member, identical with its conclusion
part.   The assumptions on which a theorem depends are present as its
hypothesis part, which is not printed explicitly but represented (as
above) by one period per formula, before the turnstile]-.

We are going to prove "FIX(FUN) == G" by computation induction; this requires that we first prove the basis "UU << G", and then as the induction step infer "FUN(F) << G" from "F << G" for arbitrary F.

```
*----------------------------------------------------------------*
|    #let th1 = MIN "G" ;;                                        |
|    th1 = ]- "UU << G" : thm                                     |
|                                                                |
*----------------------------------------------------------------*
```

(No hypothesis part this time.)

We now set up the induction formula, assume it, and complete the induction step.

```
*----------------------------------------------------------------*
|                                                                |
|    #let indform = "F << G" ;;                                   |
|    indform = "F << G" : form                                    |
|                                                                |
|    #let a2 = ASSUME indform ;;                                  |
|    a2 = .]- "F << G" : thm                                      |
|                                                                |
|    #let th2 = TRANS(APTERM"FUN"a2, a1) ;;                       |
|    th2 = ..]- "FUN F << G" : thm                                |
|                                                                |
*----------------------------------------------------------------*
```

Let us inspect the two hypotheses of the induction step.

```
*----------------------------------------------------------------*
|                                                                |
|    #hyp th2 ;;                                                  |
|    ["F << G"; "FUN G == G"] : (form list)                       |
|                                                                |
*----------------------------------------------------------------*
```

We may now apply the induction rule INDUCT. It will discharge the first of these two hypotheses.

```
*----------------------------------------------------------------*
|                                                                |
|    #INDUCT ["FUN","F"] indform (th1,th2) ;;                     |
|    .]- "FIX FUN << G" :thm ;;                                   |
|                                                                |
*----------------------------------------------------------------*
```

All that remains is to discharge the remaining hypothesis, namely "FUN G == G", and to quantify the free variables "FUN" and "G". Since we want the result to be a fact of the (draft) theory FIX, we may as well apply "newfact" immediately; it discharges all hypotheses, quantifies all free variables and then records the fact under the given name.

```
*-----------------------------------------------------*
|                                                     |
|    #newfact(`MINFIX`, it) ;;                        |
|                                                     |
|    ]- "!FUN. !G. FUN G == G  IMP  FIX FUN << G" :thm |
|                                                     |
*-----------------------------------------------------*
```

The value returned by newfact is the theorem recorded.

3.1.2 Commuting Conditions.

   We wish to prove

   ]- "!T V W X Y Z. T=>(V=>W|X)|(V=>Y|Z) == V=>(T=>W|Y)|(T=>X|Z)"

The partial session below shows how to do this by a sequence of basic
tactics, both applied separately and composed into a single (compound)
tactic. For the predefined ML types goal, simpset, proof and tactic
see Appendix 2.

```
*-----------------------------------------------------*
|                                                     |
|    #"!T V W:* X Y Z. T=>(V=>W|X)|(V=>Y|Z) ==        |
|    #                 V=>(T=>W|Y)|(T=>X|Z)" ;;       |
|    "!T ...etc... " : form                           |
|                                                     |
|    #let g = it,BASICSS,[] ;;                        |
|    g = "!T ...etc... ", -, [] : goal                |
|                                                     |
*-----------------------------------------------------*
```

The second and third components of a goal are respectively a simpset
and a form list of assumptions. Some tactics use these components in
generating goals or as part of their validations (proofs), and others
augment the components - eg by adding extra assumptions pertaining to
particular subgoals.

```
*-----------------------------------------------------*
|                                                     |
|    #let gsl,pl = GENTAC g ;;                        |
|    gsl =  [ ("!V W ...etc ... ", -, []) ] : (goal list) |
|    pl = - : proof                                   |
|                                                     |
*-----------------------------------------------------*
```

We now have a goal list with one member, and a proof (i.e. a
(thm list -> thm) function) for later use. The tactic GENTAC is the
inverse of the inference rule GEN; we want T to be a free variable
for case analysis. This is done by applying the tactic CASESTAC"T"
(CASESTAC is parameterised on a term), which gives three subgoals in
which the formula part is unchanged, but the respective assumptions
 "T==TT" , "T==FF"   and "T==UU" are added and also placed in the

simpset. It is often useful to follow CASESTAC by SIMPTAC, which simplifies the goal by the simpset and detects many tautologous goals which result.

```
*-----------------------------------------------------*
|                                                     |
|   #let gs2,p2 = (CASESTAC"T" THEN SIMPTAC)(hd gsl) ;; |
|                                                     |
|   gs2 = [ ("!V W X Y Z. UU == V=>UU|UU", -, ["T == UU"]) ] |
|                                     : (goal list)   |
|   p2 = - : proof                                    |
|                                                     |
*-----------------------------------------------------*
```

Two of the subgoals were found by SIMPTAC to be tautologies, so only one remains (the tautology checker is not quite clever enough to see that this also is a tautology). The simplest way of achieving the remaining subgoal is to repeat the sequence of tactics already used, but adjusted to perform a case analysis on V.

```
*-----------------------------------------------------*
|                                                     |
|   #let gs3,p3 =                                     |
|   #     (GENTAC THEN CASESTAC"V" THEN SIMPTAC)(hd gs2) ;; |
|   gs3 = [] : (goal list)                            |
|   p3 = - : proof                                    |
|                                                     |
*-----------------------------------------------------*
```

Now the goal list is null, so the composition of our proofs applied to the null theorem list will achieve the main goal. Note that proofs apply to theorem lists, not single theorems.

```
*-----------------------------------------------------*
|                                                     |
|   #pl[p2[p3[]]] ;;                                  |
|   ]- "!T V W X Y Z. T=>(V=>W|X)|(V=>Y|Z) ==         |
|                      V=>(T=>W|Y)|(T=>X|Z) " : thm   |
|                                                     |
*-----------------------------------------------------*
```

To shorten the task, we may use a rather general tactic which achieves (among other things) most simple laws about conditionals; it employs CONDCASESTAC as defined in Appendix 9, which does case analysis on any truth-valued term occurring as the condition of a conditional expression and containing no bound variables.

```
*-------------------------------------------------------------*
|                                                             |
|    #let CONDTAC =                                           |
|    # REPEAT(GENTAC ORELSE (CONDCASESTAC THEN SIMPTAC)) ;;   |
|    CONDTAC = - : tactic                                     |
|                                                             |
|    #CONDTAC goal ;;                                         |
|    [], - : ((goal list) # proof) ;;                        |
|                                                             |
|    #(snd it)[] ;;                                           |
|    ]- "!T V W ...etc... " : thm                            |
|                                                             |
*-------------------------------------------------------------*
```

3.1.3 A Theorem about Truth Values.

A useful theorem is the following:

]- "!B:tr. B << FF & B << TT IMP B == UU"

We will prove it here partly to illustrate the rule of contradiction
CONTR, and partly because it is used in the theory of Appendix 1. We
shall record it in the theory PPLAMB (3.4.2).

```
*-------------------------------------------------------------*
|                                                             |
|    THEORY?PPLAMB                                            |
|                                                             |
*-------------------------------------------------------------*
```

We first assume the antecedents of our theorem, and name the desired
consequent formula:

```
*-------------------------------------------------------------*
|                                                             |
|    #let asstt = ASSUME"B<<TT" and assff = ASSUME"B<<FF" ;;  |
|    asstt = .]- "B << TT" :thm                               |
|    assff = .]- "B << FF" :thm                               |
|                                                             |
|    #let w = "B == UU" ;;                                    |
|    w = "B == UU" :form                                      |
|                                                             |
*-------------------------------------------------------------*
```

We now prove that w holds under the three separate assumptions

"B == TT", "B == FF" and "B == UU" :

```
*-----------------------------------------------------------*
|                                                           |
|    #let casett = CONTR w (TRANS(SYM(ASSUME"B==TT"),assff)) |
|    #and caseff = CONTR w (TRANS(SYM(ASSUME"B==FF"),asstt)) |
|    #and caseuu = ASSUME w ;;                              |
|    casett = ..]- "B == UU" :thm                           |
|    caseff = ..]- "B == UU" :thm                           |
|    caseuu = .]- "B == UU" :thm                            |
|                                                           |
*-----------------------------------------------------------*
```

Note that each of these three theorems depends upon a case assumption,
and each of the first two depends upon one of the initial assumptions.
All that now remains is to apply the CASES rule (which will discharge
the case assumptions), and then newfact (which will discharge our
assumptions asstt and assff and quantify with respect to "B"):

```
*-----------------------------------------------------------*
|                                                           |
|    #newfact(`TRmin`, CASES"B"(casett,caseff,caseuu)) ;;    |
|    ]- "!B:tr. B << FF & B << TT  IMP  B == UU" :thm        |
|                                                           |
*-----------------------------------------------------------*
```

3.2 PPLAMBDA terms, forms and types.

PPLAMBDA is a language with two principal syntax classes: terms and forms (formulae). The terms are those of a typed \-calculus, and the forms are built from atomic forms by the normal predicate calculus connectives — conjunction (&), implication (IMP) and universal quantification (!). The atomic forms are either t == t' or t << t' , where t, t' are terms.

We are already talking in terms of concrete syntax, which you will normally use on input and see on output, and here are some examples of terms and forms which you might type or see (the full concrete syntax will be discussed in due course):

Terms:

"FF"	Constant
"G :tr->tr"	Typed function variable
"(F X)"	Application
"(P X)=>(F X)|(G(X,Y))"	Conditional expression
"\X.(G(X,Y))"	Lambda abstraction

Forms:

"TT=>X|Y == X"	Equation
"X << Y IMP F X << F Y "	Implication
"!X. X << (F X)"	Quantification

Notice that they are all quoted, using the double quotation mark. This makes them into ML expressions of metatype term and form respectively. The quotation mark (") for terms and forms is distinct from that for tokens (`) and token lists (``).

Types are also a syntax class of PPLAMBDA. They may qualify terms, as in the second example above; they may also occur as ML expressions of metatype type, preceded by a colon and within quotation marks ("). Here are some examples:

Types:

":tr"	Type constant
":*"	Type variable
":(tr,*)prod"	Cartesian product
":tr # *"	The same in infix form
":(tr,tr)fun"	Function type
":tr -> tr""	The same in infix form

Notice that type operators like prod and fun are postfixed, though some have an alternative infix.

We now proceed to give formal concrete syntax for the PPLAMBDA syntax classes.

3.2.1 Types.

Each type operator has a non-negative arity - its number of arguments. It is either predefined, or introduced with its arity by the ML function newtype (3.4.2). Nullary type operators are type constants. There are six predefined type operators, each corresponding to a domain-forming operation (see 1.3 for a brief discussion of domains):

.	(arity 0)	Domain with a single member
tr	(arity 0)	Domain of truth values TT, FF, UU:tr
u	(arity 1)	Adds a new minimum element to a domain
prod	(arity 2)	Cartesian product of two domains
sum	(arity 2)	Disjoint sum of two domains, with minimum elements coalesced
fun	(arity 2)	Continuous functions between two domains

Notice that the coalesced sum has been adopted as standard (and may be represented also by the infix +); the separated or non-coalesced sum can be expressed in terms of it and the type operator u, which is called lifting. For example

":(. u, tr u)sum"	The separated sum of ":." and ":tr"
":. u + tr u"	The same in infix form

The concrete syntax of types is as follows:

```
ty    ::=  sty              Standard (non-infix) type
        |  ty # ty          R Cartesian product
        |  ty + ty          R Disjoint sum
        |  ty -> ty         R Function space


sty   ::=  vty              Type variable
        |  id               Named type (see 3.4.3)
        |  id               Type constant
        |  tyarg id         L Compound type (with type operator id)
        |  (ty)


tyarg ::=  sty              A single type argument
        |  (ty, .. ,ty)     One or more type arguments


vty   ::=  * | ** | ..
        |  *id | **id | ..
        |  *0 | **0 | .. | *1 | **1 | ..
```

The binding power of type application (juxtaposition) and the infixes #, + and -> is decreasing, in the order given.

Every term possesses a type (forms do not possess types). Although you may decorate terms and variable binding occurrences with types (as will appear in the concrete syntax for terms) the system will attempt to infer the type of every term from three sources: (i) the generic type of each constant token (there are seventeen predefined constant tokens), (ii) the currently preferred type of each variable token (which we call its sticky type) and (iii) rules concerning what terms and forms are well-typed (which are similar to the rules for ML expressions).

3.2.2 Terms and forms.

The syntax for terms and forms is now given. We use c,bv,t,f to range over constants, binding variables, terms and forms.

```
t   ::=    c                 Constant (see 3.2.3)
       | id                  Variable
       | t t              L  Application
       | t:ty                Typed term
       | \bv.t               Lambda abstraction
       | (t)


bv ::=     id                Bound variable
       | id:ty               Typed bound variable


f   ::=    TRUTH             Tautology
       | t == t              Equation
       | t << t              Inequation
       | f & f            R  Conjunction
       | f IMP f          R  Implication
       | !bv.f               Quantification
       | (f)
```

The binding powers of application, type qualification and lambda abstraction decrease in the order given, and are less than those of the type-forming operators. Also application is left associative. Thus for example

        "\X. F G X: tr->tr"

is interpreted as

        "\X. (((F G)X):(tr->tr))"

There are some useful abbreviations:

```
"t=>u|u'"            for      "COND t u u'"
"t,t'"               for      "PAIR t t'"
"\bv1 .. bvn. t"     for      "\bv1. .. \bvn. t"
```

where the conditional operator - => - | - binds more strongly than
\ - . - , the pairing operator - , - is right associative and binds
more strongly than conditional, and the typing operator - : -   binds
more strongly than both. For example

"\X Z:tr. X=>Y|Z,W:tr"

is equivalent to

"\X. \Z:tr.(X=>Y|(Z,(W:tr)))"

The binding powers of conjunction, implication and quantification
decrease in the order given, and are less than those of the
term-forming operators. Also & and IMP associate to the right.   The
only abbreviation is

"!bvl .. bvn. f" for "!bvl. .. !bvn. f"

However, there is also some canonical reduction of forms to logically
equivalent forms. They are

"f IMP f' IMP f''" ---->   "(f & f') IMP f''"

"(f & f') & f''" ----> "f & (f' & f'')"

"TRUTH & f"   )
"f & TRUTH"   )   ----> "f"
"TRUTH IMP f"   )

"f IMP TRUTH"   )   ---->   "TRUTH"
"!v. TRUTH"   )

3.2.3 Constants, variables and well-typing.

A constant consists of a constant token c with a type, and a
variable consists of a variable token v with a type. A variable token
is an identifier. A constant token is an identifier or a single
character, excluding reserved characters like `!` etc. (`()` is a
special constant token.)

Each constant token possesses a fixed generic type,   which
determines the types at which it may occur. The role of generic types
in PPLAMBDA is close to that of generic metatypes of identifiers
declared by let or letrec in ML (2.4.2), though in PPLAMBDA they
must be stated explicitly for each new constant token introduced
(3.4.3). We indicate below how the system applies the constraint that
each occurrence of a constant token in a term or form quotation is
ascribed an instance of its generic type.

The generic types of predefined constants are as follows, where
*,** are arbitrary type variables.

Constant Token	Generic Type
TT,FF	tr
UU	*
COND	tr->*->*->*
FST	*#**->*
SND	*#**->**
PAIR	*->**->*#**
INL	*->*+**
INR	**->*+**
OUTL	*+**->*
OUTR	*+**->**
ISL	*+**->tr
FIX	(*->*)->*
UP	*->(* u)
DOWN	(* u)->*
DEF	*->tr
()	

The rules for a quoted form or term to be well-typed are as follows:

(i) Each occurrence of a constant token has a type which is some instance (by substituting types for type variables) of its generic type.

(ii) Each occurrence of a variable token has its sticky type (see below).

(iii) In every explicitly typed term t = t':ty, both t' and t have type ty.

(iv) In every application t = t'' t', if t has type ty and t' has type ty' then t'' has type ty'->ty.

(v) In every abstraction t = \bv. t', if bv has type ty and t' has type ty' then t has type ty->ty'.

(vi) In every atomic form t == t' or t << t', t and t' have the same type.

With these conventions, the system can usually provide types in quotations without any explicit types. This is more so because of the convention of sticky types. The sticky type of a variable token is the latest type which was either (i) explicitly ascribed to it in an evaluated quotation (quotations are evaluated from left to right), or (ii) possessed by it in an output quotation (again reading from left to right), or (iii) in default of (i) or (ii), inferred for it during quotation evaluation.

This convention is not applicable to constants, which may occur at different instances of their generic types - even in the same quotation. This is necessarily the case if you write for example

"UU X == UU" .

Even if X has a sticky type ":a" say, the system will not infer the types ":a->*" and ":*" for the two occurrences of "UU", since it is relevant to you which type variable is chosen. Instead it will complain that types are undetermined in the quotation. But

       "UU X == UU:*"

will suffice, or

       "UU X == UU:tr"

if a monomorphic form is what you want.

    Sticky types often save you from mentioning types explicitly, especially if you adopt different variable tokens for variables of different types. You may, for example, give sticky types to F and X by evaluating

       "F : tr ->. " , "X : tr" .

Then if Y and Z have not previously occurred as variable tokens, the evaluation of

       "F X == Y & Z << X"

will infer sticky types ":." and ":tr" for Y and Z respectively.

    Types are not normally printed in output terms and forms, but the type of any term can always be discovered; e.g. after the above you can find the type of "Z" by evaluating

       typeof "Z" .

However, if you want henceforward to see types in your output, evaluate

       typemode true ,

and to inhibit type printing later, evaluate

       typemode false .

3.2.4 Abstract syntax and antiquotation.

    The concrete syntax of PPLAMBDA constructs is purely for convenience; everything can be done (since these constructs are built only from tokens) using the abstract syntax primitives described in Appendix 4. If the user wishes to evaluate the following ML term instead of the equivalent "F X == Y & Z << X", he may do so:

```
mkconj(mkequiv(mkcomb(mkvar(`F`, mktype(`prod`, [tr;dot])),
                      mkvar(`X`, tr)),
               mkvar(`Y`, dot)),
       mkinequiv(mkvar(`Z`, tr), mkvar(`X`, tr)))
where tr = mktype(`tr`,[]) and dot = mktype(`.`,[])
```

The abstract syntax functions are intended rather for non-top-level use in procedures for manipulating syntax. You may notice that, by this means, you can compute terms or forms which disobey one of the rules for well-typing quoted phrases; for example

mkcomb(f,x) where x = "X:tr" and f = "X:tr->tr"

will evaluate to a value which is printed as "(X X)", if type printing is inhibited. These two occurrences of the token X represent distinct variables, because their types differ. If then you evaluate

mkabs("X:tr", it)

you will be given

"\X. (X X)"

but only the last occurrence of X is bound. You are not seeing the whole term, but only that part which someone would like to see who adopts distinct variable tokens at distinct types.

It is sometimes convenient to mix concrete and abstract syntax; antiquotation (denoted by ^) is useful here. Other ways of evaluating the form previously discussed are

"F^x == Y & Z << ^x" where x = "X"

or

"F X == Y & ^(mkinequiv("Z:^t", x))"
     where t = ":tr" and x = "X" .

In other words, wherever a concrete form (resp. term, type) may occur, so may ^e where e is a ML identifier or parenthesised expression of metatype form (resp. term, type).

3.2.5 Matters of style.

We have already suggested two elements of style:

(1) Adopt different variable tokens at different types. This is of mnemonic value not only to you but to the system; the sticky type is how it remembers what sort (or type) of thing your variable XZL00 stands for, so that you do not have to remind it. Of course in polymorphic forms (which may even appear as theorems) like

"!F:(*->**) G:(**->*). F(FIX(\X. G(F X))) == FIX(\Y. F(G Y))"

one wishes to use non-suggestive variable names, which may appear with other types in other forms. In these cases one may have to alter the sticky type explicitly rather often.

(2) Avoid extensive use of quotations except at top level. This is because their evaluation is inefficient (since types have to be determined).

Another suggestion:

(3) To avoid confusion between metalanguage and object language, adopt some convention (as we have here) such as

    lower case for ML identifiers (except special things
        like inference rules)
    UPPER CASE FOR PPLAMBDA VARIABLES AND CONSTANTS
    lower case for PPLAMBDA types.

3.2.6 PPLAMBDA Theorems.

We have said nothing so far in this section about inference; the terms, forms and types of PPLAMBDA are just ML data structures, and we have shown that one may compute freely with them.

By contrast, computation with theorems is more restricted. A theorem is represented by a pair consisting of its hypotheses (a form list) and its conclusion (a form); in fact it is a predeclared ML abstract type, for which we have provided only the following operations:

    destthm : thm -> (form list # form)
    hyp   : thm -> form list   For analysing theorems
    concl   : thm -> form

    printthm : thm -> thm   For output (an identity)
    newaxiom : token # form -> thm   For introducing an axiom
    newfact : token # thm -> thm   For recording a theorem

together with all the inference rules given in Appendix 5. Thus, apart from inference, one may only retrieve the component parts of theorems, or print them, or introduce them as axioms (3.4.3), or record them as part of a theory (3.4.3).

We indicated in our Introduction how this lends robustness to our system. No more need be said about theorems, since enough illustrations of inference appear in 1.1, 3.1 and Appendix 1.

3.3 Formulae which admit induction.

In the description of the rule INDUCT in Appendix 5 we state that certain formulae do not admit induction on a variable. However, most simple cases are admissible; in particular, a formula admits induction on any variable whose free occurrences are not within antecedents of implications. If you are satisfied with such cases you may safely ignore this section.

The predicate

    admitsinduction : form # term -> bool

is provided (and also used by INDUCT). The truth of admitsinduction(w,x) provides a sufficient syntactic condition for the soundness of the induction rule. In fact it implies that w is chain-complete in x; we say that w is chain-complete (cc) in x iff, whenever w is true when x stands for vi, for each member of an ascending chain of values v0,v1,..., it is also true when x stands for the limit (least upper bound) of the chain. The particular relevance is that for any continuous function f, FIX f stands for the limit of the chain whose members are denoted by UU, f(UU), f(f(UU)), ...

The predicate admitsinduction is satisfied by a fairly wide class of the pairs (w,x) for which w is cc in x. (The casual reader may prefer only to glance at the examples at the end of this section, and skip the rest). To describe the class neatly we need a few simple definitions.

First, a free occurrence of x is critical in w if it occurs within the right-hand side of an inequivalence t<<t', or within either side of an equivalence t==t'.

Second, an occurrence of a term or formula is positive (negative) in w if it is within an even (odd) number of antecedents.

Third, a type is finite if its domain is finite, and easy if its domain has no infinite ascending chains. The predicates

    finitetype, easytype : type->bool

are provided (and also used by admitsinduction). They are at present characterized as follows:

   (1) The constant types tr and . are finite and easy (in future versions of the system we shall allow you to declare constant types to be finite or easy; the present definition admits no easy types which are not also finite).

   (2) Finiteness is preserved by the type operations prod, sum, fun and u.

(3) Easiness is preserved by prod, sum and u; if ty is finite   and
ty' is easy then (ty,ty')fun is easy.

Now admitsinduction(w,x) is true exactly when

(a1) Each negative critical occurrence of x in w is such that   the
largest term containing it has easy type, and

(a2) Every quantified subformula w' = (!y...) in w containing a
free occurrence of x is such that either w' is positive in w, or
y has finite type.

Let us give some simple examples. First, wl =   "F==G IMP TT==FF"
does not in general admit induction on F, since F is negative and
critical in wl, unless F itself has easy type.

Second,   take   the   logically   equivalent   formula   w2   =
"(!Y. F(Y)==G(Y)) IMP TT==FF". Again, F is negative and critical in
w2. Now to satisfy (a1) we require the type ty' of F(Y) - the result
type of F - to be easy. However, to satisfy (a2) we also need the
type ty of Y to be finite. These two requirements are exactly the
requirement that the type ty->ty' of F is easy, in view of (3) above,
which is what we needed for the formula wl.

A rather common class of implicative induction formulae are of the
form "P(X)==TT IMP ...", where induction is required on the predicate
P. Such inductions are always admissible (at least   if   other
occurrences of P cause no problem) simply because the type tr of P(X)
is finite and hence easy.

3.4 Extending PPLAMBDA; LCF Theories.

As we said in the introduction, PPLAMBDA is not a single calculus, but a family of calculi. A member of the family is characterized by a triple (T,C,A), where T is a set of type operators each with its fixed arity, C a set of constants each with its generic type, and A a set of non-logical axioms. (Strictly we should include a fourth member - the set of named types (see 3.4.3) for abbreviating type expressions - but these have no logical significance.)

Let us think of two examples of calculi. The first - (T0,C0,A0) - we will call just PPLAMBDA; it has type constants (i.e. nullary type operators) tr and ., type operators u, prod, sum, and fun (see 3.2.1), and the constants which are listed with their generic types in Section 3.2.3. The non-logical axioms of PPLAMBDA are not explicitly present; they have been replaced by derived inference rules for pragmatic reasons (see Appendix 5). PPLAMBDA is our minimal calculus; that is, it is minimal with respect to the partial order in which (T,C,A) =< (T',C',A') iff these triples are related elementwise by set inclusion. We could indeed obtain a smaller calculus in which all three components are the nullset, but we will not consider this further (after all, we are interested in recursive functions, and for this we need at least FIX and its associated rules, to say nothing of the ubiquitous truth values and conditional).

As a second example, consider the calculus of lists given by (T,C,A) = (T0,C0,A0)u(T',C',A'), where

    T' = {list}   (a unary type operator)

    C' = { HEAD :   * list -> * ,
           TAIL :   * list -> * list ,
           CONS :   * -> * list -> * list ,
           NIL :   * list ,
           NULL :   * list -> tr ,
           REPLIST: * list -> . u + (* # * list) u ,
           ABSLIST: . u + (* # * list) u -> * list }

    A' = {]- REPLIST(ABSLIST X) == X ,
           ]- ABSLIST(REPLIST L) == L ,
           ]- HEAD L == FST(DOWN(OUTR(REPLIST L))) ,
           ]- TAIL L == SND(DOWN(OUTR(REPLIST L))) ,
           ]- CONS A L == ABSLIST(INR(UP(A,L))) ,
           ]- NIL == ABSLIST(INL(UP())) ,
           ]- NULL L == ISL(REPLIST L) }

Notice that the isomorphism between the "abstract" type * list and its "representing" type is set up explicitly by the pair of functions REPLIST and ABSLIST. These functions have to be used in defining the primitive functions over lists, but once the latter have been set up and certain common identities (such as NULL(NIL)==TT, HEAD(CONS A L)==A, etc.) proved, the definitions need never be used again. More on the theory of lists based on such identities, and a derivation of list induction, may be found in Appendix 1.

The above is nearly, but not quite, the format in which you must present the calculus to the system. We shall shortly see how to set up calculi, to name them, and to work in them. As suggested by the above example, they will often be set up by specifying extensions to one or more existing calculi.

Before going further, let us establish some terminology. Once any logical calculus is determined, so also of course is the class of all its theorems (provable sentences); this class is usually known among logicians as the _theory_ of the calculus. Indeed, we choose to talk of setting up a theory, rather than a calculus, when we determine a particular (T,C,A).

Each LCF session will be of one of two sorts, depending on your response to an initial prompt when entering the system (for which see Appendix 11). Either you will be setting up a theory - or rather, _drafting_ a theory, since the activity can be experimental and possibly abortive - or you will be working in an established theory. In the latter case, which we will discuss first since it is the simpler, you will typically prove a few theorems and record them (i.e. name them) for use in later sessions. To distinguish these recorded theorems from arbitrary theorems of the theory, we will call them _facts_.

3.4.1 Theory Structure.

Although strictly speaking each theory contains all the theories from which it was built, it is helpful to treat it as structured in the way it was built. For example, the structure

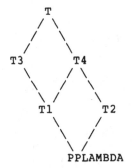

for a theory T indicates that

    T was built by extending T3 and T4
    T4 was built by extending T1 and T2, etc.

This structure is called the _parent graph_ or _ancestry_ of the theory T, and the arcs indicate the _parents_ of each theory in the ancestry. This graph is used in the storage of theories, but this need not concern you except when reading the visible record of a theory, which happens to be kept on disc files. What is more important is that each axiom and fact has a two-part name; the first part is the name of the theory in which it was introduced or proved, and the second part is its unique name within that theory.

3.4.2 Working in a theory.

To work in an existing theory T (i.e. to prove and record new facts of T), reply to the initial prompt

THEORY?

by typing T<return>. A theory name may be any token which is also an acceptable DEC10 file name, without extension.

Three functions are then available to you:

|| AXIOM : token -> token -> thm

AXIOM `T1` `AX15` gives the axiom named AX15 of theory T1. Failure if either T1 is not in the ancestry of T, or AX15 names no axiom of T1.

|| FACT : token -> token -> thm

FACT `T1` `TH15` gives the fact named TH15 of theory T1. Failure analogous to AXIOM. The token `-` may be used as first argument to AXIOM and FACT to refer to the current theory.

|| newfact : token # thm -> thm

newfact(`TH17`,th) first discharges all the hypotheses of th, makes variants of any variables whose tokens are constant tokens of T (this can occur when several theories are in the ancestry) and quantifies any free variables. The result is then recorded with name TH17 as a fact of the current theory T, and is also returned as value. Failure occurs if T already has a fact named TH17.

Notice that new facts may be recorded in any theory (while you are working in it), even one which is a parent of other theories. But once a theory is established no further types, constants or axioms may be added to it, since this could cause inconsistency with a daughter theory. Thus all the remaining functions discussed in the next section, to do with drafting theories, will fail when you are working in an established theory.

One theory is already established for you: the minimal one we called just PPLAMBDA above. To work in it, recording your own facts of this minimal theory, reply PPLAMB<return> to the initial prompt, as was done in the example of Section 3.1.3 (you may notice also that the proof of the least fixed point theorem in Section 3.1.1 could have been performed in this theory, instead of in a new draft theory). PPLAMB is implicitly a parent of every theory, so the facts you record in it may be retrieved in any theory or draft you create.

One further remark: if you are working in the theory LIST say, and using many of its axioms, it may be helpful to define

    let LISAX = AXIOM`LIST` ;;

so that "LISAX tok" may be used to abbreviate "AXIOM`LIST`tok". The same applies to facts. It is good practice to bind any such value to a ML variable to avoid repeated file access, if an axiom or fact is used many times.

3.4.3 Drafting a theory.

If you reply just <return> to the initial prompt

    THEORY?

then it is understood that you wish to draft a theory. You will then be prompted

    DRAFT?

and should reply by typing D<return>, where D is the name of your draft (again, a token which is an acceptable DEC10 file name without extension). If draft D exists already then you will continue to extend it; if not then a new draft D is created. If you reply just <return> you are working in a (new) nameless draft; in this case you will not be allowed to establish it as a theory. This default option is to be used when you do not wish to preserve any of the work of the current session for later use.

One may think of a draft as a partly specified theory; at any time the components (T,C,A) may be extended, using the functions below. The function maketheory will establish your draft as a theory; if the theory name chosen is different from the current draft name then the draft persists, and may be further extended in later sessions. Also, new facts may be recorded in a draft just as in a theory. The only restriction on a draft is that it may not become a parent, since further extension could then cause incompatibility with its daughter theories (e.g. a duplicated constant token).

The following functions are available in a draft:

|| AXIOM, FACT, newfact

These work exactly as in a theory, except that the token `-` as first argument to AXIOM and FACT now refers to the current (possibly nameless) draft, not theory.

|| newtype : int -> token -> .

The first and second arguments are the arity and identifier of a new type operator. Thus, for the operator list in the theory of lists illustrated earlier we would write

        newtype 1 `list` ;;

Failure occurs if the token is already in use as a type operator or
named type, or is not an identifier (string of letters and digits,
beginning with a letter, different from the reserved words of PPLAMBDA
syntax).

|| nametype : token # type -> .

nametype(tok,ty) introduces tok, which must be an identifier not
already in use as a type operator or named type, as an abbreviation
for ty, which must contain no type variables. Failure occurs if one
of these conditions is violated. (Note that, by contrast, a nullary
type operator, e.g. tr, is not an abbreviation.)

|| newconstant : token # type -> .

This function introduces a new constant token with its generic type.
Thus the PPLAMBDA constant FST might have been introduced by

        newconstant (`FST`, ": *#** -> * ") ;;

and the constants for the theory of lists may be introduced by

        map newconstant [`HEAD`, ":* list -> *" ;
                         `TAIL`, ":* list -> * list" ;
                         `CONS`, ":* -> * list -> * list" ;
                         `NIL` , ":* list" ;
                         `NULL`, ":* list -> tr" ;
                      `REPLIST`, ":* list -> . u + (* # * list) u" ;
                      `ABSLIST`, ":. u + (* # * list) u -> * list"] ;;

Failure occurs if the token is already a constant token, or is not an
identifier or a single character token.

|| newolinfix : token # type -> .
|| newolcinfix: token # type -> .

These functions behave just as newconstant, except that the token may
be infixed between two arguments. The functions differ in that the
arguments are paired for the first function, but curried for the
second.   Non-infixed occurrences of the constant token must be
prefixed by $. For example, if we wished to infix CONS on the theory
of lists, we would introduce it by

        newolcinfix (`CONS`, ":* -> * list -> * list") ;;

and then we would write repectively "$CONS" or "A CONS L" instead of
"CONS" or "CONS A L". But we might choose not to curry the arguments
of CONS; in that case we would introduce it instead by

```
        newolinfix (`CONS`, ":* # * list -> * list") ;;
```

and "A CONS L" now replaces "CONS(A,L)".

|| newaxiom : token # form -> thm

This function introduces an axiom for the draft.   newaxiom(`AX17`,w)
first quantifies all free variables of w and takes variants (as in
newfact) of any variables whose tokens are constant tokens, yielding
w' say.   Then]-w' is recorded with name AX17 as an axiom of the
current draft, and is also returned as result. Failure occurs if an
axiom with the same name already exists in the current draft.

    For example, the defining axiom for HEAD in the theory of lists may
be introduced (after HEAD has been introduced by newconstant) by

```
        newaxiom (`AX1`, "HEAD L == FST(DOWN(OUTR(REPLIST L)))" ) ;;
```

If you wish to use the axiom in the current session, you may then bind
it immediately to a ML variable by

```
        let HEADAX = it ;;
```

so that AXIOM `-` `AX1` (though allowed) is not needed to recover it.

    So far we have shown how to introduce the components (T,C,A) of a
draft theory from scratch.   However, if you wish to incorporate an
existing theory you may use the function

|| newparent : token -> .

The effect of

```
        newparent `T` ;;
```

is to make theory T a parent of the current draft.   Thus all types,
constants and axioms of T and its ancestors are introduced, and all
facts of T and its ancestors become accessible.

    If T is already a parent or ancestor of the current draft, its
types, constants, and axioms, will already be known and are ignored by
the call of newparent (which then has no effect); similarly for any
ancestor of T which is already an ancestor of the current draft.
Failure occurs if (1) any other type operator or named type of T is in
use for one of these purposes in the current draft, or (2) any other
constant token of T exists in the current draft, or (3) theory T does
not exist.   A call of newparent which fails has no effect on the
current draft.

|| maketheory : token -> .

The effect of

    maketheory`T` ;;

is that the current draft D is established as theory T. After the call you are then working in the theory T. If T is the same name as D (either explicitly or by use of the token `-` as argument to maketheory) then draft D dies; if not, then the draft D persists and may be extended further (in a later session) - possibly to form other theories. Failure occurs if you are working in a nameless draft, or if T is the name of an existing theory or draft (other than the current one).

3.4.4   Concrete Representation of Theories.

Theories and Drafts are held on disc files. The exact format of these files need not concern you, since you will (or should) never create such a file except through LCF. But the files are important as a visible record of your work, so it is necessary to know that a theory T is held on two files: T.THY, which is a fixed file containing all but the facts of T, and T.FCT which contains the facts of theory T you have recorded. For drafts D, the two files are D.DFT and D.FCT.

To illustrate the format of these files, which should be self explanatory, here are examples for a theory of Boolean algebra as discussed in Section 1.1:

The Theory File BA.THY

```
      THEORY BA

newtype 0 `BA` ;;

newolinfix ( `+` , ":BA#BA->BA" ) ;;

newolinfix ( `*` , ":BA#BA->BA" ) ;;

newconstant ( `-` , ":BA->BA" ) ;;

newconstant ( `0` , ":BA" ) ;;

newconstant ( `1` , ":BA" ) ;;

NEWAXIOMS();;

orcomm   "!X:BA. !Y:BA. X + Y == Y + X"

andcomm  "!X:BA. !Y:BA. X * Y == Y * X"

ordist   "!X:BA. !Y:BA. !Z:BA. X + (Y * Z) == (X + Y) * (X + Z)"

anddist  "!X:BA. !Y:BA. !Z:BA. X * (Y + Z) == (X * Y) + (X * Z)"

oride    "!X:BA. X + 0 == X"

andide   "!X:BA. X * 1 == X"

orinv    "!X:BA. X + (- X) == 1"

andinv   "!X:BA. X * (- X) == 0"
```


The Fact File BA.FCT

```
deMorgan1   "!X:BA. !Y:BA. -(X + Y) == (- X) * (- Y)"

deMorgan2   "!X:BA. !Y:BA. -(X * Y) == (- X) + (- Y)"

Doubleneg   "!X:BA. -(- X) == X"

zeroinv   "- 0 == 1"
```

LIST: An example development of a theory

In this appendix we illustrate how to set up and use theories. First we axiomatize linear lists in PPLAMBDA, next we define a derived rule of structural induction and a tactic to go with it, then finally we use this tactic to prove a simple theorem.

For completeness we present everything, including all the ML code involved. You might, at first, be surprised at how much intricate detail must be supplied by the user; however, note that:

1. The work of setting up a theory only has to be done once; therafter the various rules and tactics can be used as primitives.

2. Some of the procedures we shall program are really general purpose utilities which, had we had more foresight, might have been included with the other primitives described in the remaining appendices. It is precisely because we couldn't foresee exactly what would be needed that we made ML a general purpose programming language.

3. We have designed (but not yet implemented) an ML program which takes a specification of a structure (such as lists, trees etc - in fact anything definable by simple domain equations using the type operators +, # and u), and then automatically generates a (guaranteed consistent) axiomatization, together with a structural induction rule and structural induction tactic. Thus ML is powerful enough to automate all the intricate definitions and inferences that follow.

The remaining sections of this appendix are briefly summarized below.

Al.1: We describe a session in which we start to draft the theory LIST. We define the type `list`, the constants `HEAD`, `TAIL`, `CONS`, `NULL` and `NIL`, and various axioms about these.

Al.2: We explain how structural induction is represented as an ML function.

Al.3: We informally describe a structural induction tactic.

Al.4: We describe a session in which we set up a daughter theory of
LIST, containing the definition of a list-concatenating
function APPEND. We then prove APPEND is associative using
our structural induction tactic.

Sections Al.5 - Al.9 are concerned with setting up the induction
mechanism on which our proof depends. They can be omitted on first
reading.

Al.5: We describe a session in which a simple fact is derived (by
forward proof) from the axioms.

Al.6: We continue the session started in Al.5 by adding to LIST a
well-foundedness axiom. This axiom is needed to ensure the
validity of structural induction. We prove some more facts
and then convert the draft `LIST` into a theory.

Al.7: We program a derived cases rule which simplifies coding the
structural induction rule.

Al.8: We describe and explain the ML code for our structural
induction rule.

Al.9: We describe the ML code for our structural induction tactic.

The terminal sessions reproduced below are in the same format as
those in 2.1, except that we have slightly rearranged the system's
output, by judiciously inserting or deleting spaces and returns (this
would not have been necessary if ML had a pretty printer).

Al.1 Drafting LIST

We start by entering LCF and introducing a unary type operator
`list`.

```
*-------------------------------------------------------------*
|                                                             |
|    .RUN LCF                                                 |
|                                                             |
|    *(TML)                                                   |
|                                                             |
|    Edinburgh LCF                                            |
|                                                             |
|    THEORY?                                                  |
|                                                             |
|    DRAFT? LIST                                              |
|    (START NEW DRAFT)                                        |
|                                                             |
|    #newtype 1 `list` ;;                                     |
|    () : .                                                   |
|                                                             |
*-------------------------------------------------------------*
```

Next we introduce constants `HEAD`, `TAIL`, `CONS`, `NULL` and `NIL`:

```
*-------------------------------------------------------*
|                                                       |
|    #map newconstant                                   |
|    #    [`HEAD` , ":* list -> *"              ;        |
|    #     `TAIL` , ":* list -> * list"         ;        |
|    #     `CONS` , ":* -> * list -> * list"    ;        |
|    #     `NULL` , ":* list -> tr"             ;        |
|    #     `NIL`  , ":* list"                   ] ;;     |
|    [(); (); (); (); ()] : (. list)                    |
|                                                       |
*-------------------------------------------------------*
```

The ML functions newtype, map and newconstant are described in 3.4.3, A6c and 3.4.3 respectively. Before defining the standard axioms relating the constants it's convenient to give the PPLAMBDA variables "A" and "L" the sticky types ":*" and ":* list" (see 3.2.3). This avoids having to explicitly mention these types when we mention the variables. Since a constant (e.g. "NIL") doesn't have a sticky type, an instance of it must sometimes be given an explicit type (when not inferable from context by the system), even when the type required is identical with the generic type (see 3.2.3).

```
*-------------------------------------------------------*
|                                                       |
|    #"A:*" , "L:* list" ;;                             |
|    "A","L" : (term # term)                            |
|                                                       |
|    #map newaxiom                                      |
|    #    [`HEADax` , "HEAD(CONS A L) == A"     ;        |
|    #     `TAILax` , "TAIL(CONS A L) == L"     ;        |
|    #     `NULLax` , "NULL(CONS A L) == FF"    ;        |
|    #     `NILax`  , "NULL(NIL:* list) == TT" ] ;;      |
|    [ ]-"!A. !L. HEAD(CONS A L) == A" ;                |
|      ]-"!A. !L. TAIL(CONS A L) == L" ;                |
|      ]-"!A. !L. NULL(CONS A L) == FF";                |
|      ]-"NULL NIL == TT"              ] : (thm list)   |
|                                                       |
*-------------------------------------------------------*
```

Notice that the ML function newaxiom automatically quantifies all free variables. Axiomatizing a type as above has the disadvantage that one might introduce inconsistent sets of axioms. The ML type checker prevents invalid deductions from axioms, but it cannot prevent the user doing things like:

    newaxiom(`POWERFULax` , "TT==FF") ;;

An alternative approach, which guarantees consistency, is to define a representation of the type `list`, and a representation of the constants, and then to prove `HEADax`, `TAILax`, `NULLax` and `NILax` as theorems. A suitable representation is discussed in 3.4.

A1.2 Structural Induction

We want to program the following derived structural induction rule:

```
]- w[UU/L]
]- w[NIL/L]
]- !L.(w IMP !A. w[(CONS A L)/L])
-----------------------------------
]- !L. w
```

To represent this in ML we shall define a function:

    LISTINDUCT : term -> form -> (thm # thm # thm) -> thm

such that if:

```
UUbasis  =  ]- w[UU/L]
NILbasis =  ]- w[NIL/L]
CONSstep =  ]- !L.(w IMP !A. w[(CONS A L)/L])
```

then

    LISTINDUCT L w (UUbasis,NILbasis,CONSstep) =]- !L. w

The ML definition of LISTINDUCT is presented and explained in A1.8 below.

A1.3 The structural induction tactic LISTINDUCTAC

For goal-directed proof we shall define an ML function LISTINDUCTAC : term -> tactic, such that LISTINDUCTAC "L" is a tactic for doing structural induction on "L", more precisely:

    LISTINDUCTAC "L" g = ([g1;g2;g3] , p)

where if g = (w,ss,wl), and w is a formula with L free, then:

1. g1 = (w[UU/L],ss,wl) - the subgoal of proving w with UU substituted for L (the UUbasis case).

2. g2 = (w[NIL/L],ss,wl) - the subgoal of proving w with NIL substituted for L (the NILbasis case).

3. g3 = (w[(CONS A L)/L],ss',wl') where "A" is a new variable, ss' is ss augmented (when possible) with the induction hypothesis and wl' is wl with the induction hypothesis as an extra assumption (i.e. wl' = w.wl). This subgoal, of proving w[(CONS A L)/L] under the assumption w, deals with the

CONSstep case. Notice that, when possible, we have chosen to include the induction assumption as a simprule in the subgoal's simpset; this is not what is always wanted. The tactic LISTINDUCTAC is good for our example below, but other induction tactics might be needed in other contexts.

4. p : (thm list) -> thm is the validation function. It takes a list [th1;th2;th3] of theorems achieving goals g1, g2 and g3, and produces a theorem achieving the original goal g. This is done by feeding th1, th2 and a suitably discharged and generalised th3 to LISTINDUCT, and then specialising the result to "L".

The ML definition of LISTINDUCTAC is given in A1.9 below.

A1.4   The theory APP

We now illustrate goal-directed proof by proving the associativity of APPEND. To start with we begin a new draft called APP, which is a descendant of the theory LIST. This requires that LIST has been made a theory. This is part of the work of A1.5 - A1.9, which we assume has been done.

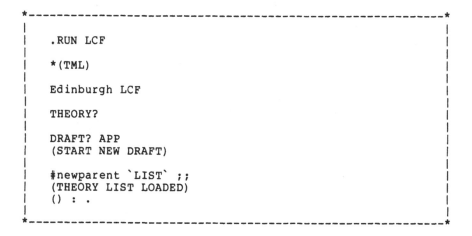

```
.RUN LCF

*(TML)

Edinburgh LCF

THEORY?

DRAFT? APP
(START NEW DRAFT)

#newparent `LIST` ;;
(THEORY LIST LOADED)
() : .
```

The call of newparent introduces the types, constants and axioms of `LIST` into the current draft, and also makes the facts of `LIST` accessible.

Next we define APPEND:

```
*------------------------------------------------------------*
|                                                            |
|    #newconstant(`APPEND` , ":* list->* list->* list") ;;   |
|    () : .                                                  |
|                                                            |
|    #"X:* list" , "Y:* list" , "Z:* list" ;;               |
|    "X","Y","Z" : (term # (term # term))                   |
|                                                            |
|    #newaxiom(`APPENDdef` ,                                 |
|    #          "APPEND X Y ==                               |
|    #              NULL X=>Y|CONS(HEAD X)(APPEND(TAIL X)Y)") ;;|
|    ]-"!X.!Y.APPEND X Y ==                                  |
|              NULL X=>Y|CONS(HEAD X)(APPEND(TAIL X)Y)" : thm|
|                                                            |
*------------------------------------------------------------*
```

Notice that we have not defined APPEND as a least fixed-point; this is because leastness is not required for the theorem we intend to prove.

Various properties of APPEND can be immediately proved by simplification, using a simpset containing the axioms of `LIST`, together with the fact]- NULL UU == UU. This, we assume, has already been proved and called `NULLfct` on the theory LIST. A session in which this is done is described in A1.5 below.

```
*------------------------------------------------------------*
|                                                            |
|    #let ss =                                               |
|    # itlist ssadd                                          |
|    #          [AXIOM `LIST` `HEADax` ;                     |
|    #           AXIOM `LIST` `TAILax` ;                     |
|    #           AXIOM `LIST` `NULLax` ;                     |
|    #           AXIOM `LIST` `NILax`  ;                     |
|    #           FACT  `LIST` `NULLfct`]                     |
|    #          BASICSS ;;                                   |
|    ss = - : simpset                                        |
|                                                            |
*------------------------------------------------------------*
```

It is convenient to define a function f : term -> thm, such that f t gives the result of simplifying (with ss) the definition of APPEND with the first quantified variable (namely "X") specialised to t.

```
*------------------------------------------------------------*
|                                                            |
|    #let f t = SIMP ss (SPEC t (AXIOM `APP` `APPENDdef`)) ;;|
|    f = - : (term -> thm)                                   |
|                                                            |
*------------------------------------------------------------*
```

Using f we can neatly prove three little lemmas:

```
*-----------------------------------------------------------*
|                                                           |
|    #let APPENDUU   = f "UU:* list"                         |
|    #and APPENDNIL  = f "NIL:* list"                        |
|    #and APPENDCONS = f "CONS(A:*)(L:* list)" ;;            |
|    APPENDUU   = ]-"!Y. APPEND UU Y == UU" : thm            |
|    APPENDNIL  = ]-"!Y. APPEND NIL Y == Y" : thm            |
|    APPENDCONS = ]-"!Y. APPEND (CONS A L) Y ==              |
|                           CONS A (APPEND L Y)" : thm       |
|                                                           |
*-----------------------------------------------------------*
```

Our goal can now be defined:

```
*-----------------------------------------------------------*
|                                                           |
|    #let g:goal =                                           |
|    # "APPEND X(APPEND Y Z)==APPEND(APPEND X Y)Z" , ssl , []|
|    #    where ssl = itlist ssadd [APPENDUU  ;              |
|    #                               APPENDNIL ;             |
|    #                               APPENDCONS]             |
|    #                               EMPTYSS ;;              |
|    g =                                                     |
|      "APPEND X(APPEND Y Z)==APPEND(APPEND X Y)Z",- ,[]     |
|        : goal                                             |
|                                                           |
*-----------------------------------------------------------*
```

We attack this goal with LISTINDUCTAC "X" followed by SIMPTAC;
is completely solves it, yielding the empty list of subgoals.
fore we can use LISTINDUCTAC we must read in its definition from the
sc, together with the definitions of the the functions it uses.
ese functions are defined in Al.7, Al.8 and Al.9 below. To read
les we use the ML function mlin, which is described in Appendix 3a.

```
*-----------------------------------------------------------*
|                                                           |
|    #map get ``CASRUL INDRUL INDTAC``                       |
|    # where get file = mlin(file,false) ;;                  |
|    ...[(); (); ()] : (. list)                              |
|                                                           |
|    #let gl , p = (LISTINDUCTAC "X" THEN SIMPTAC) g ;;      |
|    gl = [] : (goal list)                                   |
|    p = - : proof                                           |
|                                                           |
*-----------------------------------------------------------*
```

Since the empty theorem list achieves the empty goal list, we may
ly our proof function to [], to yield the desired theorem.

```
*-------------------------------------------------------------*
|                                                             |
|    #p[] ;;                                                   |
|    ]-"APPEND X(APPEND Y Z) == APPEND(APPEND X Y)Z" : thm     |
|                                                             |
|    #newfact(`APPENDassoc` , it) ;;                          |
|    ]-"!X. !Y. !Z.                                           |
|        APPEND X(APPEND Y Z) == APPEND(APPEND X Y)Z" : thm    |
|                                                             |
*-------------------------------------------------------------*
```

The rest of this appendix gives all the details omitted above;
casual readers can safely skip it.

A1.5 Forward proof of]- NULL UU == UU
(Skip on first reading)

In this section and the next we describe a session (which should
precede the one in A1.4), in which we prove the theorem
]- NULL UU == UU, and then save it as the fact `NULLfct` of LIST.
First we enter LCF and retrieve the axioms about NULL:

```
*-------------------------------------------------------------*
|                                                             |
|    .RUN LCF                                                  |
|                                                             |
|    *(TML)                                                    |
|                                                             |
|    Edinburgh LCF                                            |
|                                                             |
|    THEORY?                                                   |
|                                                             |
|    DRAFT? LIST                                              |
|    (DRAFT LIST LOADED)                                       |
|                                                             |
|    #let ax1 = SPEC "L:* list"                               |
|    #              (SPEC "A:*" (AXIOM `LIST` `NULLax`))       |
|    #and ax2 = AXIOM `LIST` `NILax` ;;                        |
|    ax1 = ]-"NULL(CONS A L) == FF" : thm                     |
|    ax2 = ]-"NULL NIL == TT" : thm                           |
|                                                             |
*-------------------------------------------------------------*
```

The specialization of `NULLax` is necessary since when a theorem
(axiom or fact) is saved on a theory (or draft) file it is closed up
by universally quantifying all free variables. We need to reestablish
the sticky types of "A" and "L" since we are in a new session. We now
prove NULLfct by first proving]- NULL UU << FF and]- NULL UU << TT,
and   then   using   modus-ponens   on   the   theorem
]- !B. B << FF & B << TT IMP B == UU. We assume this theorem has
already been proved, and saved as the fact `TRmin` of the theory
PPLAMB. (This needs to be done explicitly since the fact file of
PPLAMB is initially empty (see 3.4); a session in which `TRmin` is
proved and saved is described in 3.1.3 - we assume such a session
precedes the current one).

```
*------------------------------------------------------------*
|                                                            |
|    #let t = "NULL:* list -> tr" ;;                         |
|    t = "NULL" : term                                       |
|                                                            |
|    #let th1 = TRANS(APTERM t (MIN "CONS A L")    , ax1)    |
|    #and th2 = TRANS(APTERM t (MIN "NIL:* list") , ax2) ;;  |
|    th1 = ]-"NULL UU << FF" : thm                           |
|    th2 = ]-"NULL UU << TT" : thm                           |
|                                                            |
|    #MP (SPEC "^t UU" (FACT `PPLAMB` `TRmin`))              |
|        (CONJ(th1,th2)) ;;                                  |
|    ]-"NULL UU == UU" : thm                                 |
|                                                            |
|    #newfact(`NULLfct` , it) ;;                             |
|    ]-"NULL UU == UU" : thm                                 |
|                                                            |
*------------------------------------------------------------*
```

A1.6 Well-foundedness and the validity of Structural Induction
(Skip on first reading)

Since the only way to create theorems is via the inference rules of
Appendix 5, the function LISTINDUCT must infer]- !L. w from UUbasis,
NILbasis and CONSstep (see A1.2). Unfortunately this is not possible
from the axioms we have described so far (the curious reader might
like to construct a domain satisfying `HEADax`, `TAILax`, `NULLax` and
`NILax`, but for which structural induction fails). For structural
induction to be valid we must add another axiom asserting the
well-foundedness of lists. There are several ways of doing this; the
axiom we shall use is:

```
*------------------------------------------------------------*
|                                                            |
|    #newaxiom(`LISTax` ,                                     |
|    #          "!F. F NIL == NIL                            |
|    #              &  (!A L. F(CONS A L) == CONS A (F L) )  |
|    #              IMP (!L. F L == L)" ) ;;                 |
|    ]-"!F. F NIL == NIL                                      |
|         &  (!A. !L. F(CONS A L) == CONS A (F L) )          |
|       IMP (!L. F L == L)" : thm                            |
|                                                            |
*------------------------------------------------------------*
```

To derive structural induction from `LISTax` we must first define a
particular function LISTFUN, and then prove]- !L. FIX LISTFUN L == L.
We can then prove an induction conclusion]- !L. w follows from
assumptions UUbasis, NILbasis and CONSstep, by using fixed-point
induction (see INDUCT in A5.2e) to prove]- !L. w[(FIX LISTFUN L)/L].
The definition of LISTFUN is:

```
*------------------------------------------------------------*
|                                                            |
|    #let ty = ":(* list -> * list) -> (* list -> * list)" ;;|
|    ty = ":((*)list->(*)list)->((*)list->(*)list)" : type   |
|                                                            |
|    #newconstant(`LISTFUN` , ty) ;;                         |
|    () : .                                                  |
|                                                            |
|    #newaxiom(`LISTFUNdef` ,                                |
|    #          "LISTFUN F L ==                              |
|    #             NULL L => NIL | CONS(HEAD L)(F(TAIL L))") ;;|
|    ]-"!F. !L. LISTFUN F L ==                               |
|                  NULL L=>NIL |CONS(HEAD L)(F(TAIL L))" : thm |
|                                                            |
*------------------------------------------------------------*
```

We now prove]- !L. FIX LISTFUN L == L. We could have assumed this as an axiom instead of `LISTax`; we chose `LISTax` as we feel it is less ad-hoc and more elementary (since it contains no mention of fixed points). We start by proving, using simplification, that:

th3 =]- FIX LISTFUN NIL == NIL
th4 =]- !A L. FIX LISTFUN (CONS A L) == CONS A (FIX LISTFUN L)

The simpset we need consists of all the list axioms, together with the definition of LISTFUN.

```
*------------------------------------------------------------*
|                                                            |
|    #let ss = itlist ssadd axl BASICSS                      |
|    #          where axl = map (AXIOM `LIST`)               |
|    #                     `` HEADax                         |
|    #                        TAILax                         |
|    #                        NULLax                         |
|    #                        NILax                          |
|    #                        LISTFUNdef`` ;;                |
|    ss = - : simpset                                        |
|                                                            |
*------------------------------------------------------------*
```

For convenience we define an ML function f : term -> thm such that f t evaluates to the result of simplifying, with simpset ss, the theorem]- FIX LISTFUN t == LISTFUN (FIX LISTFUN) t (which follows from the rule FIXPT - see A5.2e):

```
*------------------------------------------------------------*
|                                                            |
|    #let f t = SIMP ss (APTHM (FIXPT "LISTFUN:^ty") t) ;;   |
|    f = - : (term -> thm)                                   |
|                                                            |
*------------------------------------------------------------*
```

Using f we can easily prove th3 and th4:

```
*-------------------------------------------------------*
|                                                       |
|   #let th3 = f "NIL:* list"                           |
|   #and th4 = GEN "A" (GEN "L" (f "CONS A L" )) ;;     |
|   th3 = ]-"FIX LISTFUN NIL == NIL" : thm              |
|   th4 = ]-"!A. !L. FIX LISTFUN (CONS A L) ==          |
|                    CONS A (FIX LISTFUN L)" : thm      |
|                                                       |
*-------------------------------------------------------*
```

Now we can prove]- !L. FIX LISTFUN L == L by specialising `LISTax` to FIX LISTFUN, and then applying modus-ponens to the result of conjoining th3 and th4.

```
*-------------------------------------------------------*
|                                                       |
|   #MP (SPEC "FIX(LISTFUN:^ty)" (AXIOM `LIST` `LISTax`)) |
|   #    (CONJ(th3,th4)) ;;                             |
|   ]-"!L. FIX LISTFUN L == L" : thm                    |
|                                                       |
*-------------------------------------------------------*
```

Finally we save our theorem as the fact `LISTFUNmin` and, now that the axiomatization of LIST is complete, convert our draft into a theory.

```
*-------------------------------------------------------*
|                                                       |
|   #newfact(`LISTFUNmin` , it) ;;                      |
|   ]-"!L. FIX LISTFUN L == L" : thm                    |
|                                                       |
|   #maketheory `LIST` ;;                               |
|   () : .                                              |
|                                                       |
*-------------------------------------------------------*
```

Note that the session described in A1.5 and A1.6 must precede the session described in A1.4.

A1.7 CONDCASES: A derived cases rule
      (Skip on first reading)

This section is a slight digression in which we define a derived rule that will come in handy for programming LISTINDUCT. The rule is:

CONDCASES : term -> form -> term -> (thm # thm # thm) -> thm
                x   w   t

If t = "t1=>t2|t3", then CONDCASES x w t is specified by:

```
tl == TT   ]-   w[t2/x]
tl == FF   ]-   w[t3/x]
tl == UU   ]-   w[UU/x]
---------------------
           ]-   w [t/x]
```

The definition of this is as follows:

```
let CONDCASES x w t (thl,th2,th3) =
let tl,t2,t3 = destcond t
in
let case tv = SYM(SUBSOCCS [[l],SYM(ASSUME "^tl==^tv")]
                          (CONDCONV(mkcond(tv,t2,t3))))
in
CASES tl (SUBST [case "TT"    ,x] w thl,
          SUBST [case "FF"    ,x] w th2,
          SUBST [case "UU:tr",x] w th3) ;;
```

We shall not explain this definition here (since it is just general ML programming). We assume that the definition of CONDCASES has been placed on the disc file CASRUL; this is read in during the session described in A1.4.

A1.8 Programming LISTINDUCT
   (Skip on first reading)

We can now program the rule LISTINDUCT which we specified and discussed in A1.2. Here is the definition, we explain it later:

```
let LISTINDUCT L w (UUbasis,NILbasis,CONSstep) =
let () , [ty] = desttype(typeof L)
in
let fty = ":^ty list -> ^ty list"
in
let basis' = GEN L (SUBST [SYM(MINAP "(UU:^fty)^L"),L] w UUbasis)
and F      = genvar fty
in
let w' = "!^L.^(substinform ["^F ^L" , L] w)"
in
let thl = SPEC "^F(TAIL ^L)" CONSstep
and th2 = SPEC "TAIL ^L" (ASSUME w')
in
let th3 = SPEC "HEAD ^L" (MP thl th2)
and t   = "NULL ^L => NIL | CONS(HEAD ^L)(^F(TAIL ^L))"
in
let th4 = CONDCASES L w t (NILbasis,th3,UUbasis)
and th5 = INSTTYPE [ty,":*"] (AXIOM `LIST` `LISTFUNdef`)
in
let step' = GEN L (SUBST [SYM(SPEC L (SPEC F th5)),L] w th4)
in
let th6 = INDUCT ["LISTFUN:^fty->^fty",F] w' (basis',step')
and th7 = INSTTYPE [ty,":*"] (FACT `LIST` `LISTFUNmin`)
in
GEN L (SUBST [(SPEC L th7),L] w (SPEC L th6)) ;;
```

We assume this definition resides on the disc file INDRUL; this is read in during the session described in A1.4. To see how the definition of LISTINDUCT works, assume:

```
UUbasis  = ]- w[UU/L]
NILbasis = ]- w[NIL/L]
CONSstep = ]- !L.(w IMP !A. w[(CONS A L)/L])
```

Then we trace through a call

```
LISTINDUCT L w (UUbasis,NILbasis,CONSstep)
```

as follows:

1. ty is the type of the elements of the lists being inducted on.

2. fty is the type (ty list -> ty list).

3. basis' =]- !L.w[(UU L)/L].

4. F is a new variable of type fty.

5. w' = !L.w[(F L)/L].

6. th1 =]- w[F(TAIL L)/L]. IMP !A.w[CONS A (F(TAIL L))/L].

7. th2 = !L. w[(F L)/L]]- w[F(TAIL L)/L].

8. th3 = !L. w[(F L)/L]]- w[CONS(HEAD L)(F(TAIL L))/L].

9. t = NULL L => NIL | CONS(HEAD L)(F(TAIL L)).

10. th4 = !L. w[(F L)/L]]- w[t/L].

11. th5 is the type instance of the polymorphic axiom LISTFUNdef obtained by instantiating ":*" to ty.

12. step' = !L. w[(F L)/L]]- !L. w[LISTFUN F L/L].

13. th6 =]- !L. w[(FIX LISTFUN L)/L].

14. th7 is the type instance of LISTFUNmin obtained by instantiating ":*" to ty.

15. Finally, the result is:]- !L. w

Each time LISTINDUCT is called the above proof is performed, computing]- !L. w by inference.

A1.9 Programming LISTINDUCTAC
      (Skip on first reading)

The ML definition of LISTINDUCTAC is:

```
let LISTINDUCTAC L (w,ss,wl) =
let tok , [ty] = desttype(typeof L)
in
let A = (variant("A:^ty",goalfrees)
          where goalfrees = union(form1frees wl,formfrees w))
in
let   UUcase = substinform ["UU:^ty list" ,L] w
and  NILcase = substinform ["NIL:^ty list",L] w
and CONScase = substinform ["CONS ^A ^L"   ,L] w
and      ss' = (ssadd (ASSUME w) ss) ? ss
and      wl' = w.wl
and        p = \[th1;th2;th3].
                 SPEC L (LISTINDUCT L w (th1,th2,th)
                      where th = GEN L (DISCH w (GEN A th3)))
in
([(UUcase,ss,wl);(NILcase,ss,wl);(CONScase,ss',wl')] , p) ;;
```

We assume this definition resides on the disc file INDTAC; this is
read in during the session described in A1.4.

Predeclared ML types

In addition to the basic ML types

```
          ., int, bool, token    (elementary types)
          term, form, type       (types pertaining to PPLAMBDA)
```

and the type operators

```
          list                   (unary)
          #, +, ->               (binary, infixed)
```

there are two predeclared abstract types (2.4.5) in the system. The first is thm; the operations available on theorems are:

```
    destthm : thm -> form list # form
        hyp : thm -> form list
      concl : thm -> form
   printthm : thm -> thm
   newaxiom : token # form -> thm
    newfact : token # thm -> thm
```

together with all the PPLAMBDA inference rules in Appendix 5. The second is simpset; the available operations (see also Appendix 8) are:

```
    EMPTYSS : simpset
    BASICSS : simpset
      ssadd : thm -> simpset -> simpset
     ssaddf : (term -> term # thm) -> simpset -> simpset
    ssunion : simpset -> simpset -> simpset
   simpterm : simpset -> term -> term # thm
   simpform : simpset -> form -> form # (thm->thm) # (thm->thm)
```

Many other functions (for example SIMPTAC) have been defined in terms of these.

There are also three predeclared defined types (2.4.4):

```
       goal = form # simpset # form list
      proof = thm list -> thm
     tactic = goal -> (goal list # proof)
```

Primitive ML Identifier Bindings

   The basic functions of ML over the types in Appendix 2 are
provided as predeclared identifiers of the language. These are of two
kinds: (a) bindings of ordinary identifiers, and (b) bindings of
dollared identifiers (see Section 2.2.3) formed by prefixing $ to
(some) infix and prefix operators. This appendix lists the types, and
failure conditions where applicable, of the primitive operations that
do not involve PPLAMBDA objects (those pertaining to PPLAMBDA and the
use of the system for proofs are given in Appendices 4, 5, 7, 8 and 9,
and in Sections 3.3 and 3.4); further general-purpose ML functions are
listed in Appendix 6. For many below we omit description of the
function to which the identifier is bound as this should be clear from
the identifier name and type given. For those functions whose
application may fail, the failure token is the function identifier.

   Predeclared identifiers are not, however, regarded as constants of
the language. As with all other ML identifiers, the user is free to
rebind them, by let, letref, etc., if he wishes (but note that, in the
case of infix or prefix operators, rebinding the dollared operator
will affect even its non-dollared uses). Their predeclared bindings
are to be understood as if they had been bound by let (rather than
letref); in particular, therefore, none of them can be changed by
assignment (except, of course, within the scope of a rebinding of the
identifier by a letref-declaration).

(a) Predeclared ordinary identifiers.

```
    fst :  * # ** -> *
    snd :  * # ** -> **

    null: * list -> bool
    hd  : * list -> *          || fails if arg is the null list
    tl  : * list -> * list     || fails if arg is the null list

    inl :  * -> * + **
    inr :  ** -> * + **
    outl: * + ** -> *          || fails if arg not in left-summand
    outr: * + ** -> **         || fails if arg not in right-summand
    isl : * + ** -> bool

    explode: token -> token list
    implode: token list -> token
```

   explode maps a token into the list of its single character tokens
   in order; implode maps a list of single character tokens (fails
   if any token is of length different from one) into the token
   obtained by concatenating these characters. For example:

```
        explode `whosit` = ``w h o s i t``
        implode ``c a t`` = `cat`
        implode ``cd ab tu`` = failwith `implode`
```

```
gentok :  . -> token
```

Each time it is called, gentok returns a new token which is not
equal to any previously used token (or, indeed, to any ML token
that might be used in the future). Such tokens are intended
principally for internal use in computations; they have a
printname (of the form Gnnnn where each n is a digit) which you
may see on output, but this cannot be used to input them.

```
tokofint :  int -> token
intoftok :  token -> int
```

These are bound to the obvious type transfer functions, with
intoftok failing if its argument is not a non-negative integer
token.

```
mlinfix :  token -> .
mlcinfix:  token -> .
```

mlinfix declares its argument token to the ML parser as having
infix status, so that function applications involving this token
may be written using infix notation; thus, after

```
        mlinfix `plus` ;;
        let $plus(x,y) = x+y ;;
```

then, e.g., 1 plus 2 is synonymous with $plus(1,2). Similarly,
mlcinfix declares its argument token as having curried-infix
status, and after

```
        mlcinfix `curriedplus` ;;
        let $curriedplus x y = x+y ;;
```

then 1 curriedplus 2 is synonymous with $curriedplus 1 2 .
[Note: Only ordinary identifiers and certain single character,
non-digit, non-layout tokens can be used as infixes or
curried-infixes; infixing other tokens would have unpredictable
effect on the parser.]

```
mlin :  token # bool -> .
```

mlin(tok,prflag) reads and evaluates ML phrases from the file
named tok on the user's disk area exactly as if they had been
typed by the user at top-level. The first argument, tok, can be
any acceptable DEC10 filename with or without extension (with
failure for unacceptable filenames and for non-existent files).
The second argument determines the printing of results; with
prflag=true these are printed as usual at top-level, while with
prflag=false a single period is printed for every top-level
phrase successfully read and evaluated. If any failure occurs
during loading, the call of mlin fails without the rest of the
file being read. Additionally, whether successful or not, a call

of mlin automatically ends any section begun by loading the file but not explicitly ended.
[Note: calls of mlin can be nested, i.e. a file being input by mlin can itself contain calls of mlin.]

```
printbool :   bool -> bool
printint  :   int -> int
printtok  :   token -> token
printdot  :   . -> .
printterm :   term -> term
printform :   form -> form
printtype :   type -> type
printthm  :   thm -> thm
```

These are all identity functions with the side effect of printing their argument exactly as they would be printed at top-level.

(b) Predeclared dollared identifiers.

Those corresponding to the following operators are provided:

```
do            :   * -> .
not           :   bool -> bool
*, /, +, -    :   int # int -> int
>, <          :   int # int -> bool
=             :   * # * -> bool
@             :   * list # * list -> * list        (list append)
.             :   * # * list -> * list             (list cons)
```

Clarifying remarks:

1. $do is equivalent to $(\x.())$. [See also Section 2.3.2.]

2. $/ returns the integer part of the result of a division, e.g.

    $$\$/(7,3) = 7/3 = 2$$
    $$\$/(-7,3) = -7/3 = -2$$

    The failure token for division by zero is `div`.

3. $- is the binary subtraction function. Negation (unary minus) is not available as a predeclared function of ML, only as a prefix operator; of course, the user can define it if he wishes, e.g. by

    let minus x = -x ;;

4. Not all dollared infix operators are included above: $, is not provided since it would be equivalent (as a function) to the identity on pairs, nor is $& as it has no corresponding call-by-value function (because e & e' evaluates to false when e does even if evaluation of e' would fail to terminate), nor is $or analogously.

5. $= is bound to the expected predicate for an equality test at
non-function types, but is necessarily rather weak, and may give
surprising results, at function types.   You can be sure that
semantically (i.e. extensionally) different functions are not
equal, and that semantically equivalent functions are equal when
they originate from the same evaluation of the same textual
occurrence of a function-denoting expression; for other cases the
equality of functions is unreliable (i.e. implementation
dependent). For example, after the top-level declarations

```
        let f x = x+1
        and g x = x+2 ;;
        let f' = f
        and h x = f x
        and h' x = x+1 ;;
```

f=f' is true and f=g is false, but the truth values of f=h, f=h',
and h=h' are unreliable; further, after declaring

```
        let plus = \x.\y.x+y ;;
        let f = plus 1
        and g = plus 1 ;;
```

the truth value of f=g is also unreliable.

Primitive ML Functions for PPLAMBDA

This appendix lists the ML constructors and destructors dealing with the abstract syntax of PPLAMBDA. These are the primitive functions for the ML types type, term, form, and thm. All other syntactic functions are definable with these (see Appendix 7).

For all failures below, the failure token is the function identifier.

A4.1 Type primitives.

The objects of ML type type are the type expressions of PPLAMBDA. More precisely, they are those types which do not contain named types; the latter are purely for abbreviation of types on input and output.

(a) Constructors.

```
mkvartype  :  token -> type
mktype     :  token # type list  ->  type
```

Notes:
    1. The token for mkvartype must be a sequence of one or more *'s, followed possibly by a numeral or identifier.
    2. The token for mktype must be a currently known type operator, and the length of the type list must be equal to its arity.

(b) Destructors.

```
destvartype  :  type -> token
desttype     :  type -> token # type list
```

Notes:
    1. desttype will fail on a type variable, and destvartype will fail in all other cases.
    2. As implied above, desttype will act on a named type exactly as it acts on the type named.

A4.2 Term primitives.

The terms are those of the typed \-calculus determined by the constants and types of the theory under consideration.

For abstractions and combinations, note that the constructors below do not require a type as an argument (the constructor fails if types are not compatible). Similarly, the corresponding destructors return a result which does not include the type of the term. (The function typeof in Appendix 7 enables you to find their type when you need.)

(a) <u>Constructors</u>.

```
mkabs   : term # term -> term
mkcomb  : term # term -> term
mkvar   : token # type -> term
mkconst: token # type -> term
```

Notes:
1. mkabs(t,t') fails if t is not a variable.
2. mkcomb(t,t') fails if the type of t is not a function type tyl->ty2 with tyl equal to the type of t'.
3. mkvar(tok,ty) fails if tok is a constant of the current theory.
4. mkconst(tok,ty) fails unless tok is a constant of the current theory and ty is an instance of its generic type.

(b) <u>Destructors</u>.

```
destabs   : term -> term # term
destcomb  : term -> term # term
destvar   : term -> token # type
destconst: term -> token # type
```

These all fail on terms belonging to the wrong phyla.

A4.3 <u>Form primitives</u>.

In the present LCF system, we have elected to build in some formula identifications corresponding to some "trivially valid" equivalences between forms. This is done by canonicalizing forms, as follows:

1. implications are eliminated in favour of conjunctions by

    w IMP (w' IMP w'')   --->   (w & w') IMP w''

2. conjunctions are regrouped to be right associative:

    (w & w') & w''   --->   w & (w' & w'')

3. occurrences of TRUTH as subforms are eliminated by

!x.TRUTH	--->	TRUTH
TRUTH & w	--->	w
w & TRUTH	--->	w
TRUTH IMP w	--->	w
w IMP TRUTH	--->	TRUTH

These canonicalizations are propagated by the constructors mkimp, mkconj, and mkquant below. However, the corresponding destructors do not reverse the process (as it cannot be unique in the reverse direction);   all   the   destructors fail on forms whose surface decomposition is not of the right kind.

(a) Constructors.

```
mkquant  :  term # form -> form
mkimp    :  form # form -> form
mkconj   :  form # form -> form
mkequiv  :  term # term -> form
mkinequiv:  term # term -> form
mktruth  :  . -> form
```

Notes:
  1. mkquant(t,w) fails if t is not a variable.
  2. mkequiv(t,t') fails if t, t' are not of the same type.
     Similarly, for mkinequiv.

(b) Destructors.

```
destquant  :  form -> term # form
destimp    :  form -> form # form
destconj   :  form -> form # form
destequiv  :  form -> term # term
destinequiv:  form -> term # term
desttruth  :  form -> .
```

A4.4 Theorem primitives.

There is only one, for obtaining the components of a theorem:

destthm : thm -> form list # form

wl]- w   ]--> (wl,w)

No corresponding constructor is provided, as the creation of theorems is confined to the application of axioms (or axiom schemes) or inference rules [see next appendix and Section 3.4 on theories].

PPLAMBDA Inference Rules

The paper "A Logic for Computable Functions with Reflexive and Polymorphic Types" (see Bibliography) gave the logical rules and axioms of LCF and its non-logical axioms. However, early investigations with a direct implementation of these showed that they often lead to long and expensive proofs. In place of the non-logical axioms we choose to provide as ML primitives a collection of derived rules and axiom schemes. One change from the original axiomatisation is that we have now adopted coalesced sums and lifting as standard type operators, where previously separated sums were used; apart from this, and pragmatic convenience, the present collection is logically equivalent to the original (i.e. the same theorems follow as consequences).

In general, an inference rule can be viewed as a function which takes some number of theorems as arguments (the hypotheses of the rule), returning a theorem as result (the conclusion of the rule). However, many are really rule schemes, requiring parameters, and this is reflected in their types below by allowing for additional arguments of type term or form. (In some cases this is not, strictly speaking, necessary since the appropriate term or formula could - though with some difficulty and extra computation - be deduced by analysing the theorems supplied as hypotheses; but it is pragmatically justified as this information will generally be readily available in the context in which one wishes to use the rule and allows extra checks to be built into its use, e.g. when programming many of the standard tactics listed in Appendix 9. In one case below, however, note that two versions, SUBST and SUBS, of the substitutivity rule are available, one requiring parameters (and doing extra checking, etc.), the other not.)

Similarly, most axioms - rules without hypotheses - become axiom schemes in our current system; these take only non-theorem arguments and return a theorem as result. Since often (in fact, in all axiom schemes below except ASSUME) only one parameter of type term is needed, for this appendix we introduce the defined type axscheme given by

        lettype axscheme = term -> thm

To help shorten the description of each function below, we shall adopt the following format and conventions:

(1) First, we give the type of the function implementing the axiom or rule, and, for rules with parameters, under each parameter position in its type we introduce a metavariable, chosen as follows:

```
t, u, v    for    terms
    w      for    (well-formed) forms
    x      for    terms expected to be variables
    f      for    variables usually of function type
```

When a term parameter is expected to be a variable by this convention, the rule fails if applied with a term as actual parameter which is not a variable.

(2) The pattern of inference effected by a rule is shown in the customary manner for sequent calculi, with hypotheses above a line and conclusion below the line. For rules with a list of theorems as hypotheses, only the typical i-th member of the list is shown (e.g. in SUBST, thi should be of the form Ai]- ti ==ui).

(3) For rules with more than one hypothesis, the order of these above the line is intended to correspond with the order of arguments of type thm given in the type of the rule.

(4) All rules fail if applied to theorems not of the form shown for their hypotheses.

(5) In displaying the rules, A is used as a metavariable for sets (of type form list) of formulae occurring as assumptions of theorems, and u is used to denote the operation for forming unions of assumptions (e.g. in CONJ, SUBST, CASES below).

(6) A different format is used for showing the functional behaviour of an axiom scheme, since this depends on a finer analysis of its (non-theorem) parameters. We give a list of mutually exclusive cases (often there is only one) in a "maps to" notation ... |--> ... using metavariables as in (1). For example, a case might be

$$t \ x \quad |--> \quad (some theorem)$$

This case applies when the actual parameter is a term matching the pattern on the left (i.e., for this example, a combination with a variable as its rand), and then t and x denote its rator and rand, respectively, throughout the theorem on the right. In some axiom schemes so displayed, we write ".." in the theorem on the right of a case to stand for the term on the left.

(7) All axiom schemes fail if no case applies.

(8) Following each rule or axiom scheme, any failure conditions not implied in (1), (4), or (7) are listed.

(9) For all failures, the failure token is the function identifier.

(10)   Substitution of t for u (not necessarily a variable)   throughout
a term or formula X is denoted below by X[t/u], and simultaneous
substitution of tl for ul, t2 for u2, ..., and tn for un is denoted
by X[...ti/ui...], with these operations taking variants of bound
variables as necessary [see Appendix 7(g)].

(11)   In some rules, =< is used to stand for == or << (the same at
each occurrence within a rule).

Other points to note:

1.   In forming unions of assumptions of theorems, u does not notice
alpha-convertibility;   this is left to be treated on discharging
an assumption.

2.   Note that most rules below are provided as "curried" functions,
taking non-theorem parameters first and theorems (generally, as a
tuple when more than one) later. This is particularly convenient
for working in a goal-directed manner via tactics, where the
non-theorem parameters are generally known when a tactic is
applied whereas the arguments of type thm are only supplied when
performing the proof-function component of a successful tactic.

A5.1   Logical rules and axioms.

These consist of the standard ones for the sequent predicate
calculus, plus two rules for (simultaneous) instantiation of variables
and type variables, respectively, in theorems.

(a) Axioms. There is one axiom, AXTRUTH, expressing the basic
property of the nullary predicate symbol TRUTH, and one axiom
scheme, ASSUME, for assuming a formula:

$$AXTRUTH : thm =]-TRUTH$$

$$ASSUME : form \rightarrow thm \qquad w \mid\rightarrow \{w\}]-w$$

(b) Introduction rules.

CONJ : thm # thm -> thm   (conjunction)

$$\frac{A1 \ ]- \ w1 \qquad A2 \ ]- \ w2}{A1 \ u \ A2 \ ]- \ w1 \ \& \ w2}$$

GEN : term -> thm -> thm   (generalization)
     x

$$\frac{A \ ]- \ w}{A \ ]- \ !x.w}$$

Failure condition: x occurs free in A

```
DISCH : form -> thm -> thm              (discharging an assumption)
         w
                        A ]- w'
                        --------------
                        A' ]- w IMP w'

              where  A' is the set of assumptions
                     in A not alpha-convertible to w
```

(c) <u>Elimination</u> <u>rules</u>.

```
SEL1, SEL2 :   thm -> thm                               (selection)

              A ]- w1 & w2            A ]- w1 & w2
              ------------            ------------
                A ]- w1                 A ]- w2

         where  w1 is neither a conjunction or TRUTH
                (because of formula identification - see A4.3)
```

```
SPEC :   term -> thm -> thm                        (specialization)
           t
                        A ]- !x.w
                        -----------
                        A ]- w[t/x]

         Failure condition:  t and x of different type
```

```
MP :   thm -> thm -> thm                            (modus ponens)
                 A1 ]- mkimp(w,w')      A2 ]- w
                 ------------------------------
                        A1 u A2 ]- w'
```

The ML constructor, mkimp, is used here to indicate that, for MP,
we provide an inference rule which extends the usual one for modus
ponens by allowing a more generous decomposition of its hypotheses
which notices formula identification. To be more precise, suppose
thimp = A1]- wimp and th = A2]- w. Then, MP(thimp)(th) is
defined so that, for a successful application, it does not require
that wimp is literally w IMP w' (for some w') but only that this
holds up to formula identification (including the special cases
where either of w,w' may be TRUTH). For example, if wimp is
w1 & w2 IMP w3 and w is w1, then MP(thimp)(th) returns
A1 u A2]- w2 IMP w3.

(d) Instantiation rules.

```
INST :   (term # term) list -> thm -> thm
           ti     xi
```

$$
\frac{A\ ]-\ w}{A\ ]-\ w[...ti/xi...]}
$$

Failure condition: any xi occurs free in A.


```
INSTTYPE :   (type # type) list -> thm -> thm
               tyi    vtyi
```

$$
\frac{A\ ]-\ w}{A\ ]-\ w\{...tyi/vtyi...\}}
$$

where in the (simultaneous) instantiation w{...tyi/vtyi...} of
types tyi for vartypes vtyi throughout w, the rule makes a
variant (with primes) of any variable which would otherwise
become identical with any other variable, including those in
A. (See also instinform in Appendix 7.)

```
    Failure conditions:  1. any vtyi is a vartype in A
                         2. any vtyi is not a vartype
```

A5.2 Non-logical rules and axioms.

(a) Basic properties of == and <<.

```
SYNTH :  thm # thm -> thm                      (synthesis of ==)
```

$$
\frac{A1\ ]-\ t << u \qquad A2\ ]-\ u << t}{A1\ u\ A2\ ]-\ t == u}
$$

```
ANAL :  thm -> thm                             (analysis of ==)
```

$$
\frac{A\ ]-\ t == u}{A\ ]-\ (t << u)\ \&\ (u << t)}
$$

```
HALF1, HALF2 :  thm -> thm            (= SEL1 o ANAL, SEL2 o ANAL)
```

$$
\frac{A\ ]-\ t == u}{A\ ]-\ t << u} \qquad \frac{A\ ]-\ t == u}{A\ ]-\ u << t}
$$

```
REFL :   axscheme                                (reflexivity of ==)

              t  |-->    ]- t == t

SYM :   thm -> thm                               (symmetry of ==)
                         A ]- t == u
                         -----------
                         A ]- u == t


TRANS :   thm # thm -> thm                        (transitivity)

                Al ]- t =< u        A2 ]- u =<' v
                ----------------------------------
                     Al u A2 ]- t =<'' v

     where   =<'' is == if both =< and =<' are, otherwise <<


SUBST :(thm # term) list -> form -> thm -> thm       (substitutivity
       thi     xi           w                             of =)

                Ai ]- ti == ui        A' ]- w[...ti/xi...]
                ------------------------------------------
                   Union(Ai) u A'  ]- w[...ui/xi...]


SUBS :   thm list -> thm -> thm

                Ai ]- ti == ui        A' ]- w
                ------------------------------
                Union(Ai) u A' ]- w[...ui/ti...]


SUBSOCCS :   (int list # thm) list  -> thm -> thm
                occli      thi

         As for SUBS, but substitutes only for (free) occurrences  of
         ti   whose   occurrence   number   belongs   to  occli  [see
         substoccsinform in Appendix 7].
```

(b) <u>Rules</u> <u>connected</u> <u>with</u> <u>term</u> <u>formation</u>.

```
APTERM :   term -> thm -> thm                    (apply t to both
             t                                    sides of an =<)

                        A ]- u =< v
                        ---------------
                        A ]- t u =< t v

    Failure condition:  t u (or, equivalently, t v) not
                        a well-typed combination


APTHM :   thm -> term -> thm                      (apply both sides
             t                                     of an =< to t)

                        A ]- u =< v
                        ---------------
                        A ]- u t =< v t

    Failure condition:  u t (or v t) not a well-typed combination


LAMGEN :   term -> thm -> thm
             x

                        A ]- u =< v
                        -----------------
                        A ]- \x.u =< \x.v

    Failure condition:  x occurs free in A
```

(c) <u>Lambda-conversion</u> <u>and</u> <u>extensionality</u>.

```
BETACONV :   axscheme

             (\x.u)v     |-->    ]- (\x.u)v == u[v/x]


ETACONV :    axscheme

             \x.(u x)    |-->    ]- \x.(u x) == u

    Failure condition:  x occurs free in u
```

```
EXT :  thm -> thm                        (extensionality of =<)

                     A ]- !x. u x =< v x
                     -------------------
                       A ]- u =< v

      Failure condition:  x occurs free in u or v


ABS :  term -> thm -> thm
         x

                     A ]- u x =< t
                     -------------
                     A ]- u =< \x.t

      Failure condition:  x occurs free in u or in A
```


(d) <u>Minimality of UU</u>.

```
  MIN :  axscheme              t    |-->    ]- UU << t

  MINAP :  axscheme            UU t |-->    ]- UU t == UU

  MINFN :  axscheme           \x.UU |-->    ]- \x.UU == UU
```


(e) <u>Properties of FIX</u>.

```
  FIXPT :  axscheme

             fun    |-->     ]- FIX fun == fun(FIX fun)

      Failure condition:  type of fun not a funtype
                          ty -> ty' with ty = ty' .

  FIX :  thm -> thm

                     A ]- t == FIX fun
                     -----------------
                     A ]- t == fun t
```

```
INDUCT :  (term # term) list -> form -> (thm # thm) -> thm
           funi    fi           w

    A1 ]- w[...UU/fi...]        A2 u {w} ]- w[...funi(fi)/fi...]
    ----------------------------------------------------------
                  A1 u A2 ]- w[...FIX(funi)/fi...]

    Failure conditions: 1. some fi occurs free in A2
                        2. typeof of some funi not a funtype
                           tyi -> tyi' with tyi = tyi'
                        3. w does not admit induction on some fi
                           [See Section 3.3]
```

(f) <u>Properties</u> <u>of</u> <u>DEF,</u> <u>COND</u> <u>and</u> <u>the</u> <u>truth</u> <u>value</u> <u>domain.</u>

```
AXDEF :   axscheme

                t         |-->        ]- DEF t << TT


DEFUU :  thm -> thm

                    A ]- DEF t == UU
                    ----------------
                    A ]- t == UU


DEFCONV :  axscheme

              DEF UU          |-->       ]- .. == UU
              DEF ()          |-->       ]- .. == UU
              DEF TT          |-->       ]- .. == TT
              DEF FF          |-->       ]- .. == TT
              DEF(UP t)       |-->       ]- .. == TT
              DEF(ISL t)      |-->       ]- .. == DEF t
              DEF(INL t)      |-->       ]- .. == DEF t
              DEF(INR t)      |-->       ]- .. == DEF t
              DEF(OUTL t)     |-->       ]- .. == (ISL t => TT | UU)
              DEF(OUTR t)     |-->       ]- .. == (ISL t => UU | TT)


CONDCONV :  axscheme

              TT=>t|u         |-->       ]- .. == t
              FF=>t|u         |-->       ]- .. == u
              UU=>t|u         |-->       ]- .. == UU
```

CONDTRCONV : axscheme

```
              COND TT      |-->      ]- .. == \X.\Y.X
              COND FF      |-->      ]- .. == \X.\Y.Y
              COND UU      |-->      ]- .. == UU
```

CASES : term -> (thm # thm # thm) -> thm
         t

```
     Alu{t==TT} ]- w     A2u{t==FF} ]- w    A3u{t==UU} ]- w
     ---------------------------------------------------------
                        Al u A2 u A3 ]- w
```

CONTR : form -> thm -> thm
        w

$$A\ ]-\ tl\ =<\ t2$$
$$\text{-------------}$$
$$A\ ]-\ w$$

when (1) tl and t2 are distinct members of {"UU:tr","TT","FF"}
and (2) if tl is "UU" then the connective is "==".

Failure condition: (1) or (2) above is violated.

(g) Axiom scheme for the one-point domain.

  DOT : axscheme

```
            t          |-->      ]- t == ()
```

  Failure condition: t not of type ":."

.(h) Lifted domains: properties of UP and DOWN.

  DOWNCONV : axscheme

```
            DOWN(UP t)      |-->      ]- .. == t
            DOWN UU         |-->      ]- .. == UU
```

  UPCONV : axscheme

```
            UP(DOWN t)        |-->      ]- DEF t == TT IMP  .. == t
```

(i) <u>Product</u> <u>domains:</u> <u>selection</u> <u>and</u> <u>pairing</u>.

   SELCONV : axscheme

```
            FST(t,u)      |-->      ]- .. == t
            SND(t,u)      |-->      ]- .. == u
             FST UU       |-->      ]- .. == UU
             SND UU       |-->      ]- .. == UU
```

   PAIRCONV : axscheme

```
            (FST t, SND t)    |-->    ]- .. == t
               (UU,UU)        |-->    ]- .. == UU
```


(j) <u>Sum</u> <u>domains:</u> <u>injection,</u> <u>projection,</u> <u>and</u> <u>discriminators</u>.

   ISCONV : axscheme

```
               ISL(INL t)     |-->    ]- .. == DEF t
               ISL(INR t)     |-->    ]- .. == (DEF t => FF | UU)
                 ISL UU       |-->    ]- .. == UU
```

   OUTCONV : axscheme

```
               OUTL(INL t)    |-->    ]- .. == t
               OUTR(INR t)    |-->    ]- .. == t
               OUTL(INR t)    |-->    ]- .. == UU
               OUTR(INL t)    |-->    ]- .. == UU
                 OUTR UU      |-->    ]- .. == UU
                 OUTL UU      |-->    ]- .. == UU
```

   INCONV : axscheme

```
               INL(OUTL t)    |-->    ]- ISL t == TT IMP  .. == t
               INR(OUTR t)    |-->    ]- ISL t == FF IMP  .. == t
                 INL UU       |-->    ]- .. == UU
                 INR UU       |-->    ]- .. == UU
```

(k) <u>Simplification</u>.

```
SIMP :   simpset -> thm -> thm
           ss
```

$$\frac{A \;]- \; w}{A \; u \; A' \;]- \; w'}$$

where w' (= fst(simpform ss w)) is the result of simplifying
w using equivalences in ss as left-to-right replacement
rules, and A' is a subset of the hypotheses of the
theorems in ss [see simpform in Appendix 8].

General Purpose and List Processing Functions

This appendix describes some commonly useful functions applicable
to pairs, lists, and other ML values. All are definable in ML; for
each function we give, in addition to its type, an ML declaration
equivalent to that defining it in the current system. Those preceded
by $ may be used either as infix operators (without the $) or as
functions (with the $).

(a) General purpose functions.

```
I :  * -> *
K :  * -> ** -> *
pair: *-> ** -> * # **
```

These are defined by

```
let I x = x ;;
let K x y = x ;;
let pair x y = (x,y) ;;
```

can : (* -> **) -> * -> bool   (test for failure)

can(f)(x) applies f to x, returning true if this evaluation
succeeds and false otherwise; can is equivalent to

```
let can f x = (f x ; true) ? false ;;
```

$o : (** -> ***) # (* -> **) -> (* -> ***)

$o(f,g), or equivalently f o g , returns the functional
composition of f and g, given by

```
let $o(f,g) x = f(g x)  ;;
```

$# : (* -> ***) # (** -> ****) -> ((* # **) -> (*** # ****))

$#(f,g) combines f and g to yield the function on pairs
determined by applying f and g to its components:

```
let $# (f,g) (x,y) = ( f x , g y )  ;;
```

(b) List searching functions.

The following functions search lists for elements with various
properties; those returning elements fail if no such element is
found, those returning boolean results never fail.

    find : (* -> bool) -> * list -> *

    find(p)(l) returns the first element of l which satisfies the
    predicate p; find is equivalent to

            letrec find p l = null l => fail |
                               p(hd l) => hd l
                                   | find p (tl l) ;;

    tryfind : (* -> **) -> * list -> **

    tryfind(f)(l) returns the result of applying f to the first member
    of l for which application of f succeeds; tryfind is equivalent to

            letrec tryfind f l = null l => fail
                               |(f(hd l) ? tryfind f (tl l)) ;;

    exists : (* -> bool) -> * list -> bool
    forall : (* -> bool) -> * list -> bool

    exists(p)(l) applies p to the elements of l in order until one is
    found which satisfies p, or until the list is exhausted, returning
    true or false accordingly; exists is equivalent to

            let exists p l = can (find p) l ;;

    forall is equivalent to

            let forall p l = not(exists ($not o p) l)   ;;

    mem : * -> * list -> bool

    mem(x)(l) returns true if some element of l is equal to x,
    otherwise false; mem is equivalent to

            let mem x l = exists (\y.x=y) l ;;

    genmem : (* # ** -> bool) -> * -> ** list -> bool

    genmem(p)(x)(l) returns true if p(x,y) holds for some element y of
    l, otherwise false; genmem is equivalent to

            let genmem p x l = exists (\y.p(x,y)) l   ;;

```
assoc :    * -> (* # **) list -> (* # **)
revassoc : ** -> (* # **) list -> (* # **)
```

assoc(x)(l) searches the list l of pairs for one whose first
component is equal to x, returning the first pair found as result;
similarly, revassoc(y)(l) searches for a pair whose second
component is equal to y. assoc and revassoc are equivalent to

```
let assoc x l = find (\(x',y).x=x') l
and revassoc y l = find (\(x,y').y=y') l ;;
```

Examples: assoc 2 [(1,4);(3,2);(2,5);(2,6)] = (2,5)
              revassoc 2 [(1,4);(3,2);(2,5);(2,6)] = (3,2)

(c)   **List mapping and iterating functions.**

```
map :  (* -> **) -> * list -> ** list
```

map(f)(l) returns the list obtained by applying f to the elements
of l in turn; map is equivalent to

```
letrec map f l = null l => [] | f(hd l).map f (tl l) ;;
```

```
itlist :   (* -> ** -> **) -> * list -> ** -> **
revitlist : (* -> ** -> **) -> * list -> ** -> **
```

For arguments f, l, and x, these two functions perform iterated
compositions of the curried function f, using elements of l as
first arguments of f; x is used for the second argument of the
first call of f, thereafter the result of each call is passed as
second argument of the next call. itlist is characterised by

```
itlist f [l1;l2;...;ln] x = f l1 (f l2 (...(f ln x)...))
                          = ((f l1) o (f l2) o...o (f ln)) x
```

revitlist is similar but reverses the order of the composition:

```
revitlist f [l1;...;ln] x = ((f ln) o...o (f l1)) x
```

In ML, itlist and revitlist are equivalent to

```
letrec itlist f l x = null l => x | f(hd l)(itlist f (tl l) x);;

letrec revitlist f l x = null l => x
                              | revitlist f (tl l) (f(hd l)x) ;;
```

(d)   List transforming functions.

```
  rev :  * list -> * list

    rev(l) reverses the list l; rev is equivalent to

          let rev l = revl(l,[])
                    whererec revl(l,l') = null l => l'
                                        | revl(tl(l), hd(l).l') ;;


  filter :  (* -> bool) -> * list -> * list

    filter(p)(l) applies p to every element of l, returning a list  of
    those which satisfy p; filter is equivalent to

          letrec filter p l = null l => []
                            |(let l' = filter p (tl l)
                             in  p(hd l) => hd(l).l' | l' ) ;;


  mapfilter :  (* -> **) -> * list -> ** list

    mapfilter(f)(l) applies f to every element of l, returning a  list
    of results for those elements for which application of f succeeds;
    mapfilter is equivalent to

          letrec mapfilter f l = null l => []
                               |let l' = mapfilter f (tl l)
                                in  (f(hd l).l') ? l'      ;;


  intersect :  * list # * list -> * list
  subtract :  * list # * list -> * list
  union :  * list # * list -> * list

    These three provide the obvious functions on sets  represented  as
    lists without repetitions;  they are equivalent (for all lists) to

          let intersect(l1,l2) = filter (\x.mem x l2) l1
          and subtract(l1,l2) = filter (\x.not(mem x l2)) l1
          and union(l1,l2) = l1 @ subtract(l2,l1)  ;;


  flat :  (* list) list  ->  * list

    flat(ll) flattens a list of lists, and is equivalent to

          letrec flat ll = null ll => [] | hd(ll) @ flat(tl ll) ;;
```

```
split  :  (* # **) list  ->  (* list) # (** list)
combine:  (* list) # (** list)  ->  (* # **) list
```

These two map a list of pairs into the corresponding pair of
lists, and conversely, respectively (with combine failing if its
argument lists are not of the same length); they are equivalent to

```
letrec split l = null l => (nil,nil)
                 |let (x1,x2).l' = l
                  in let l1',l2' = split l'
                     in ( x1.l1' , x2.l2' )

and combine (l1,l2) =
        null l1 => (null l2 => nil | failwith `combine`) |
        null l2 => failwith `combine`
      | let (x1.l1'),(x2.l2') = l1,l2
        in  (x1,x2).combine(l1',l2')  ;;
```

(e) **Miscellaneous**.

nil : * list

The identifier nil provides an alternate syntax for the null list:

```
let nil = [] ;;
```

length : * list -> int

length is equivalent to

```
letrec length l = null l => 0 | 1 + length(tl l) ;;
```

PPLAMBDA Syntax Functions

This appendix defines ML identifier bindings for the basic
syntactic   functions   -   predicates,   selectors,   tests   for
alpha-convertibility, substitution, term and formula matching, etc. -
provided for objects of type term, form, and type. For many of these
the type discipline of ML makes it necessary to provide different
functions for terms and forms, and (where appropriate) for types and
for form lists; in these circumstances we shall describe only the
function for terms, the others being analogous.

(a) Discriminating predicates.

Each primitive destructor listed in Appendix 4 determines a
corresponding predicate which returns true or false according as the
destructor succeeds or fails;   e.g. isquant can be defined by

            let isquant = can destquant ;;

The following predicates (one for each syntactic alternative, or
phylum, and all defined like isquant) are provided:

            isquant   )
            isimp   )
            isconj   )
            isequiv   ) : form -> bool
            isinequiv)
            istruth   )

            isabs   )
            iscomb) : term -> bool
            isvar   )
            isconst)

            isvartype : type -> bool

(b) Phylumof functions.

Often more useful than the predicates given in (a) are the
following two functions mapping terms and formulae, respectively, to a
token identifying the phylum to which they belong (the result token
always being one of those listed):

    phylumofterm : term -> {`abs`, `comb`, `const`, `var`}
    phylumofform : form -> {`quant`, `imp`, `conj`,
                            `equiv`, `inequiv`, `truth`}

Together with the failure mechanism of ML, these functions enable one to adopt a natural "case-switch" style, particularly for programming functions defined by structural induction. For example, the function termvars listed in (e) below may be defined by

```
let termvars t =
        failwith phylumofterm t
        ??``const`` nil
        ??``var``  [t]
        ??``abs``  (let x,u = destabs t in
                        union([x], termvars u) )
        ??``comb``  (let u,v = destcomb t in
                        union(termvars u, termvars v) ) ;;
```

Because the two phylumof functions are implemented to be particularly quick, this style of programming will generally be more efficient, and more readable, than other alternatives (e.g., via iterated conditional tests using the predicates in (a), or by successive use of the primitive destructors and failure trapping until one succeeds).

(c) Selectors.

At present only the following selectors have been provided (the user can easily define others, e.g. rator, rand, etc., if he wishes):


```
lhs :  form -> term
rhs :  form -> term
```

lhs returns the left-hand side of an inequivalence or equivalence (similarly, rhs returns the right-hand side) and fails on other forms; they are equivalent to

```
let lhs w = fst(destequiv w ? destinequiv w)
and rhs w = snd(destequiv w ? destinequiv w) ;;
```

```
hyp  :  thm -> form list
concl:  thm -> form
```

hyp and concl return the assumptions and conclusion, respectively, of a theorem; they are equivalent to

```
let hyp = fst o destthm
and concl = snd o destthm ;;
```

```
typeof : term -> type
```

typeof maps (well-typed) terms to their types; it is equivalent to

```
letrec typeof t =
        failwith phylumofterm t
            ??``const``  snd(destconst t)
            ??``var``  snd(destvar t)
            ??``abs``  (let x,u = destabs t in
                            mktype(`fun`, [typeof x; typeof u]) )
            ??``comb``  (let u,v = destcomb t in
                            let (),[();ty] = desttype(typeof u) in
                            ty   ) ;;
```

(d) Compound constructors and destructors.

Again only a few are provided; the ones listed are included
mainly because they were used in implementing some of the inference
rules in Appendix 5. For brevity, we describe their functional
behaviour via the case notation used in Appendix 5.

```
mkcond :  term # term # term -> term

        t1, t2, t3        |-->        t1 => t2 | t3
                                      [i.e. COND t1 t2 t3]

    Failure conditions: 1. t1 not of type ":tr"
                        2. t2 and t3 not of the same type


mkpair :  term # term -> term

        t1, t2        |-->        (t1,t2)
                                  [i.e. PAIR t1 t2]


destcond :  term -> term # term # term

        t1 => t2 | t3      |-->        t1, t2, t3
        [i.e. COND t1 t2 t3]
        other terms        |-->     failwith `destcond`


destpair :  term -> term # term

        (t1,t2)        |-->        t1, t2
        [i.e. PAIR t1 t2]
        UU:ty1#ty2     |-->        UU:ty1, UU:ty2
        other terms    |-->     failwith `destpair`
```

(In the second case, ty1 and ty2 are used as metavariables for
types; this case reflects the fact that the least pair (UU,UU) is
the least element of a product domain.)

(e) <u>Functions</u> <u>connected</u> <u>with</u> <u>variables</u> <u>and</u> <u>type</u> <u>variables</u>.

   variant : term # term list -> term

     variant(x,l) primes or unprimes x as many times as necessary to
     obtain a variable not equal to any variable occurring in l.
        (Note on equality of variables: Two variables are equal iff
     they consist of the same token with the same type; thus, e.g.,
     "X:tr" and "X:." are different variables.)

   genvar : type -> term

     Each time it is called, genvar(ty) creates (via gentok) a new
     variable of type ty which is not equal to any previously used
     variable. Such variables are for internal use only (c.f. gentok
     in Appendix 3).

   termvars, termfrees   :   term -> term list
   formvars, formfrees   :   form -> term list
   formlvars, formlfrees :   form list -> term list

     termvars(t) returns a list of all variables in t; termfrees(t)
     returns a list consisting only of those variables which occur free
     in t. (Note: both return sets, i.e. lists without repetitions.)

   termtyvars : term -> type list
   formtyvars : form -> type list
   typetyvars : type -> type list
   formltyvars: form list -> type list

     termtyvars(t) returns a list of all type variables occurring in
     the type of any subterm of t.

(f) <u>Alpha-convertibility</u>, <u>freeness</u> <u>and</u> <u>typesin</u> <u>predicates</u>.

   aconvterm : term # term -> bool
   aconvform : form # form -> bool

     aconvterm(t,t') returns true is t is alpha-convertible
     to t', otherwise false.

   freeinterm : term list -> term -> bool
   freeinform : term list -> form -> bool

     An occurrence of a term t (not necessarily a variable) as a
     subterm of a term u is said to be <u>free</u> <u>in</u> <u>u</u> if all free
     occurrences of variables in t are free occurrences of these
     variables in the whole term u. freeinterm(l)(u) returns true if a

term alpha-convertible to any member of the term list 1 occurs free in u, otherwise false.

```
Example: Let   t  = "X(\Y.X Y)"
               ul = "X(\Y.X Y)(X Y)"   (= "^t (X Y)" )
               u2 = "\X.X(\Y.X Y)"     (= "\X.^t" )
Then
               freeinterm[t]ul = true
               freeinterm[t]u2 = false
```

```
typesinterm :   type list -> term -> bool
typesinform :   type list -> form -> bool
typesintype :   type list -> type -> bool
```

typesinterm(tyl)(t) returns true or false according as any type in tyl occurs in the type of any subterm of t or not.

(g) <u>Ordinary substitution</u>.


```
substinterm :   (term # term) list -> term -> term
substinform :   (term # term) list -> form -> form
```

substinterm[(tl',tl);---;(tn',tn)](u) returns the result of simultaneously, for i=1,---,n, substituting ti' for all free occurrences of (subterms alpha-convertible to) ti in u, making variants of bound variables as necessary to prevent free occurrences of variables in ti' becoming bound in the result; that is, when u is an abstraction \x.v with tl occurring free in v and x occurring free in tl' but not in tl, the result is

```
      \x'. substinterm [tl',tl] (substinterm [x',x] v)
      where  x' = variant(x, 1)
               where 1 = union(termfrees tl', termfrees u)
```

Failure condition: ti' and ti not of the same type for some i.
                   (The failure token for both substinterm
                    and substinform is `substin`.)


```
substoccsinterm :   (term # int list # term) list -> term  -> term
substoccsinform :   (term # int list # term) list -> form  -> form
```

substoccsinterm[(tl',occll,tl);---;(tn',occln,tn)](u) substitutes ti' only for those free occurrences of ti in u whose occurrence number (counting from left to right) belongs to occli (which should be an ordered list without repetitions).

Failure condition and failure token: as for substinterm

Example: If   u = "F X (\X.X) X X"
          then
              substoccsinterm ["TT",[1;3],"X"] u = "F TT (\X.X) X TT"

(h) Type substitution (instantiation).

    instintype :   (type # type) list -> type -> type
    instinterm :   (type # type) list -> term -> term
    instinform :   (type # type) list -> form -> form

    instinterm[(tyl',tyl);---;(tyn',tyn)](t)   simultaneously,   for
    i=1,---,n, substitutes tyi' for tyi throughout t, making a variant
    of any variable which would otherwise become identical to any
    other variable in the result.

The latter condition on instinterm arises, as with ordinary
substitution, from the need to prevent capture of bound variables (and
from the obvious desire that type instantiation should commute with
alpha-conversion). This is illustrated by

Example 1:
    If   t = "\X:*.F(X:a)(X:*)"
    then
          instinterm [":a",":*"] t = "\X':a.F(X:a)(X':a)"

If here such variants were not taken, the free occurrence of X:a would
become bound in the result.

For more complex terms, sometimes several different variants are
necessary, when several diffferent variables all change and become
identical as a result of the instantiation.   In these circumstances,
instinterm makes variants so that changed variables (whether free or
bound) which were different before the instantiation remain different
in the result (with all occurrences of the same variable becoming
occurrences of the same variant, of course). An example of this is

Example 2:
    If   t = "\X:a->*.F(X:a->a)(X:a->*)(X:*->*)(X:a->*)"
    then
          instinterm [":a",":*"] t
          = "\X':a->a.F(X:a->a)(X':a->a)(X'':a->a)(X':a->a)"

(Note that none of these complications for type instantiation
arise if you adopt a discipline for variable names which ensures that
the terms and formulae never involve the same variable token at
different types, but the system functions must make some decision
about how to treat such an eventuality.)

(i) <u>Printing</u> <u>of</u> <u>terms</u> <u>and</u> <u>forms</u>.

   typemode : bool -> bool

     typemode is an identity function with the side effect of setting a
     flag controlling the printing of types in output terms and forms;
     typemode(true) enables printing of complete type information,
     while typemode(false) inhibits type printing.   [See also Section
     3.2.3.]

(j) <u>Term</u> <u>and</u> <u>formula</u> <u>matching</u>.

   termmatch : term -> term -> (term # term) list
   formmatch : form -> form -> (term # term) list

     termmatch(p)(t) tries to find a (simultaneous) substitution, of
     terms for variables, which when applied to p yields t, failing if
     none exists; more precisely, it returns, when successful, a list

        [(u1,x1); (u2,x2); ---; (un,xn)]

    of term-variable pairs such that

       (i) substinterm [(u1,x1);(u2,x2);---;(un,xn)] (p) = t , and

       (ii) the variables x1,x2,...,xn are pairwise distinct and all
           occur free in p (to eliminate redundant pairs and ensure
           the result is unique).

Simplification

Although fully automatic proof procedures are beyond the immediate
aims of LCF, proof generation would be extremely laborious without
some ability to have simple inferences made automatically.
Simplification is one such step towards reducing the effort involved
for the user and is the only standardized element of automatic proof
in the present system.

To invoke simplification of a term or formula, the user supplies a
set of equivalences - generally theorems already proved, or local
assumptions - to be used as simplification rules; the system
functions respond with a simplified term or formula, together with a
proof justifying the simplification.

From the user's point of view, sets of simplification rules form
an abstract type simpset. The following abstract type declaration
summarises the available primitives on simpsets (others, e.g. for
listing simpsets or for removing rules from simpsets, are likely to be
added later):

    abstype simpset = . . .

      with simpterm : simpset -> term -> term # thm = . . .

      and simpform : simpset -> form -> form # (thm->thm) # (thm->thm)
                                                            = . . .
      and ssadd : thm -> simpset -> simpset = . . .

      and ssaddf : (term->term#thm) -> simpset -> simpset = . . .

      and ssunion : simpset -> simpset -> simpset = . . .

      and EMPTYSS : simpset = . . .

      and BASICSS : simpset = . . .

The functions simpterm and simpform and the choice of their types
will be explained in Sections 2 and 3, after describing in Section 1
how equivalences are used as simplification rules. One rarely needs
to use simpterm and simpform explicitly as such but will usually
invoke simplification via the standard tactic SIMPTAC (see next
appendix); SIMPTAC is defined in terms of simpform.

EMPTYSS and BASICSS are simpset constants, the former consisting
of no simplification rules, the latter containing standard rules for
beta conversion, conditionals, minimality of UU, etc. Section 4 gives
the full list of standard rules for PPLAMBDA presently included in
BASICSS.

A8.1 Simplification rules.

Informally, an equivalence p == p' determines a simplification rule by regarding p as a pattern - of variables and type variables - to be matched against subterms of a term or formula to be simplified. When the match succeeds, a subterm t which is an instance of the left-hand side p may then be replaced by the corresponding instance t' of the right-hand side p'. However, since we then want also a proof of t == t' , some care is required to take account of the assumptions used in proving p == p'.

Specifically, suppose we have proved p == p' under a set of assumptions A; that is, we have a theorem th of the form

(1)   A]- p == p'

Then the required care is that, when attempting to match p to a term t, instantiations are allowed only for

   (a) variables free in p but not in A, and
   (b) type variables occurring in p but not in A.

To see the purpose of restriction (a) - the reason for (b) is analogous - suppose we can obtain t from p by substitution of u for x, and let t' = p'[u/x]. When x is not free in A, we can prove t == t' from th via the inference rule INST ; that is, evaluating INST[u,x]th will yield the theorem

                    A]- t == t'

This theorem is then acceptable as justification for the replacement of t by t' as it involves only assumptions which were made earlier, outside simplification (so there is no need to establish them during simplification, as they will presumably be discharged or proved elsewhere). But if x occurs free in A, the above inference is invalid, and the call of INST will fail, for the good reason that t == t' would then hold only under hypotheses A[u/x]; permitting variables (or type variables) which are the subject of current assumptions to be instantiated in this way would contravene the natural deduction style in which assumptions are carried through unchanged until discharged.

Sometimes, however, one does want to include as a simplification rule an equivalence dependent on hypotheses with which it shares variables and type variables. (In practice, the most common examples are usually that the term instantiated for a variable in the equivalence should satisfy some simple condition such as being a strict function, or a non-null list, or belongs to a particular summand of a sumtype.) For doing this, any theorem of the form

(2)   A]- w IMP p == p'

can be used as a conditional simplification rule. Replacement of an instance of p is then permitted only if the corresponding instance of the antecedent w is first proved by simplification (a theorem justifying the replacement then following by Modus Ponens). Again variables and type variables in A may not be instantiated, and for pragmatic reasons - to prevent too many unprovable instances of w being attempted - we add one further constraint: that every term, v say, instantiated for variables in w should be free in the context of its occurrence in the whole term or formula being simplified, i.e. no free occurrence of a variable in v is bound in the whole term or formula being simplified. (A similar constraint on types instantiated for type variables in w is not needed as there is no binding operator in PPLAMBDA for type variables.)

With these considerations in mind, the function

> ssadd :   thm -> simpset -> simpset

will accept for inclusion in a simpset any theorem of the form (1) or (2) above, or whose conclusion is any quantification of these (the latter to relieve the user of routine quantifier stripping). Thus, the general form of theorems accepted is

$$A \;]\!- \{!\underline{x}\} \; (\{w \; IMP\} \; p == p')$$

where the braces indicate optional parts and $\underline{x}$ is a vector of variables. For theorems not of this form, ssadd fails with token `ssadd`.

Occasionally simplification rules are not expressible (at least, not conveniently) as theorems to be used as unrestricted replacement patterns. This is the case, for instance, if one wishes to limit instantiations in the left hand side by constraints expressible only metalinguistically (e.g. that the term instantiated for a variable should be a constant, or that only monotyped instances are to be permitted). For such purposes, there is an operation

> ssaddf :   (term->term#thm) -> simpset -> simpset

on simpsets for including any user-supplied function

> funsr :   term -> term # thm

which maps satisfactory terms t to a term t' together with a theorem A]- t == t'   justifying a replacement; during simplification the standard package will try funsr on all subterms t, allowing replacement by t' provided the theorem is of the form indicated.

Notice that one way of obtaining such functional simplification rules is by partially applying simpterm (see below) to a simpset argument only, which may have its uses (for parcelling up subsets of simplification rules as local simplifiers). The function termmatch (see Appendix 7(j)) may also be noted as convenient for user-programming of pattern-directed functional simplification rules.

The function

ssunion : simpset -> simpset -> simpset

combines two simpsets.

A8.2 Simplification of terms.

The function

simpterm : simpset -> term -> term # thm

simplifies terms by repeatedly applying members of the simpset to the term and all its subterms, in some order (in fact, "top-down, rators-before-rands" in the present implementation), until no further simplification is possible. In addition, simpterm composes together (with TRANS, APTERM, APTHM and LAMGEN) the instances of theorems in the simpset used along the way to prove an equivalence justifying its simplifications.

More precisely, simpterm(ss)(t) returns a pair (t',th) where t' is the full simplification of t by ss as just indicated and th is a theorem of the form

wl]- t == t'

The restriction mentioned earlier on free variables and type variables of hypotheses ensures that wl is always a subset of hyps(ss), the hypotheses of theorems in ss. (In fact, wl will be exactly the union of the hypotheses of those members of ss used during the simplification.)

When no simplification is possible, simpterm(ss)(t) does not fail but returns t with the proof of]- t == t by reflexivity.

A8.3 Simplification of forms.

Forms are simplified by simplifying all their subterms. In addition, the following subforms are detected as tautologies:

1. equivalences and inequivalences which follow trivially by reflexivity (more precisely, atomic forms t =< t' for which t is alpha-convertible to t'),

2. inequivalences UU << t which are instances of MIN,

3. inequivalences which follow from MIN by monotonicity and transitivity (e.g. f UU << f x , g(h x UU)UU << g(h x y)z , etc.).

4. implications   wal & ... & wam IMP wcl & ... & wcn   in
   which every conjunct wcj in the consequent is
   alpha-convertible to some conjunct wai in the antecedent.

5. implications   wal & ... & wam IMP wc   in which some
   conjunct wai is a standard contradiction (i.e. of the form
   expected by the inference rule CONTR in Appendix 5).

These tautologies are reduced to TRUTH, which then propagates in the
form by the formula identifications of Appendix 4; that is,

```
    !x.TRUTH        simplifies to    TRUTH
    TRUTH & w       simplifies to    w
    w & TRUTH       simplifies to    w
    TRUTH IMP w     simplifies to    w
    w IMP TRUTH     simplifies to    TRUTH
```

One further refinement is added for implications. When asked to
simplify an implication   wal & ... &wam IMP wc , simpform will
detect some equivalences in the antecedent and include them in the
simpset for tackling the consequent wc.   Some limitation must be
imposed, however, on such automatic additions to simpsets,   in
particular to ensure that equivalences are used the right way round as
simplification rules. We eschew an attempt at a general treatment
(say, via measure-decreasing functions on terms) for now and limit
simpform to detecting only the most common case: equivalences,
possibly quantified, in which exactly one side is a constant (usually
one of "TT", "FF" or "UU" in practice). The non-constant side of the
equivalence is then taken as the left-hand side (by using the
inference rule SYM if necessary) of a simplification rule for wc.

The ML function, simpform, performing these simplifications
differs from simpterm in that the "proof" component of the result
returned by simpform is quite different in character to that returned
by simpterm.   When w simplifies to w', we want, in addition to w', a
proof that w is equivalent to w', and this poses a slight problem as
there is no biconditional connective (iff) in PPLAMBDA.   One
alternative would be to return a theorem which proves

$$(w \text{ IMP } w') \ \& \ (w' \text{ IMP } w) \qquad ,$$

but then the canonicalization (see A4.3) of forms makes simpform
rather clumsy to use.

We choose instead to have simpform return two functions f and f'
mapping theorems (generally with hypotheses, of course) proving w and
w', respectively, into a theorem proving the other.   Thus, simpform
has the type

```
simpform : simpset -> form -> form # (thm->thm) # (thm->thm)
```

and is defined so that, when w simplifies to w' as outlined above,

```
simpform(ss)(w) = (w',f,f')   where   f :  ]-w  |-->  ]-w'
                              and     f': ]-w' |-->  ]-w
```

Concerning hypotheses, the functions f and f' may return in general theorems with extra hypotheses but, as for simpterm, only ones belonging to hyps(ss). More precisely, then, for all wl,

$$f : \quad wl \;]- w \quad |--> \quad wl' \;]- w'$$

with wl' a subset of the union of wl and hyps(ss). Similarly for f'.

A8.4 Standard simplification rules in BASICSS.

BASICSS includes simplification rules for PPLAMBDA corresponding to each axiom scheme in Appendix 5 which is a conditional conversion scheme. By a conditional conversion scheme, we mean any function

$$CONV : \quad term \rightarrow thm$$

which maps satisfactory terms t (with failure for other terms) to a theorem

$$]- \{w \; IMP\} \; t == t'$$

with empty hypotheses, the curly brackets indicating an optional condition w. Such schemes will allow replacement of t by t' provided the antecedent w (when present) is first proved by simplification. The full list BASICSS knows about is

1. \-calculus conversion: BETACONV, ETACONV
2. minimality of UU :   MINAP, MINFN
3. truth-valued constants: DEFCONV, CONDCONV, CONDTRCONV
4. lifted domains: UPCONV, DOWNCONV
5. selection and pairing: SELCONV, PAIRCONV
6. sum domain conversions: ISCONV, OUTCONV, INCONV

Standard Tactics and Tacticals

A9.1 Goals and Theorems

In Section 2.5 we discussed goals and events in general, and in 2.5.3 we discussed a particular type of goal defined by

    lettype goal = form # simpset # formlist

Our standard tactics are written for this kind of goal, with theorems as events. The intention is that, if g = (w,ss,wl), then a tactic may use both the simpset ss and the assumptions wl in attempting to prove w; if it produces subgoals it may add both simplification rules to ss and assumptions to wl in doing so.

The achievement relation between theorems and goals was also defined in 2.5.3. For this relation we claim that all the standard tactics below are valid. (However, for a tactic which takes a theorem parameter - e.g. the induction and substitution tactics - the hypotheses of the theorem parameter must be counted as assumptions of the goal.) In fact they are also strongly valid (with the exception of induction), which is to say that whenever a goal is achievable so are all the subgoals produced.

Our standard tactics are in no sense a complete set; we have selected those which were most useful in our case studies.

A9.2 Standard Tactics.

We have predefined

    lettype proof = thm list -> thm
    lettype tactic = goal -> (goal list # proof).

In describing tactics below we write

    g |---> [g1;...;gn]

to indicate the goallist produced for a typical goal g, ignoring the proof part. Some tactics are parameterized; the extra arguments are "curried" and precede the goal argument. The failure token is always the tactic name.

All these tactics are written in ML; many of them are inverses, in some sense, of a single inference rule.

CASESTAC : term -> tactic

```
t |---> (w,ss,wl) |--->
              [ (w, ss1, "^t==TT".wl) ;
                (w, ss2, "^t==FF".wl) ;
                (w, ss3, "^t==UU".wl) ]
```

where ss1, ss2 and ss3 are simpsets with the respective new assumptions added as simplification rules. Failure if t is not of type tr.

CONDCASESTAC : tactic

Finds some condition t (i.e. a term of type tr occurring as the condition of a conditional expression) which is free in the form of the goal, and applies CASESTAC(t). Failure when there is no such t.

GENTAC : tactic

```
(!x.w, ss, wl) |---> [ (w[x'/x], ss, wl) ]
```

where x' is a variant of x not free in wl. Failure if the goal form is not quantified.

SUBSTAC : thm list -> tactic

```
..]-ti==ui |---> (w,ss,wl) |---> [ (w[...ui/ti...], ss, wl) ]
```

Failure if any thm argument is not an equivalence.

SUBSOCCSTAC : (int list # thm) list -> tactic

Just like SUBSTAC, except that for each i-th pair in the list the first component [n1;..;nk] specifies the free occurrences (in left-to-right order) of ti in w to be replaced by ui.

SIMPTAC : tactic

```
(w,ss,wl) |---> [ (w',ss,wl) ]
```

where w' is the simplification of w by ss, except that if w' is a simple tautology (see Appendix 8) then the subgoal list is null. No failure.

INDUCTAC : thm list -> tactic

```
..]-ti==FIX(ui) |---> (w,ss,wl) |--->
              [ (w[...UU/ti...], ss, wl) ;
                (w[...ui(xi)/ti...], ss, w[...xi/ti...].wl) ]
```

where each xi is a variable (a variant of ti if ti is a variable) which is not free in w or wl. Notice that the inductive hypothesis is added to the assumption list. Failure if the thm arguments are not of the form given.

INDUCOCCSTAC : (int list # thm) list -> tactic

> Just like INDUCTAC, except that for each i-th pair in the list the first component [nl;..;nk] specifies the free occurrences in left-to-right order) of ti in w to be the subject of induction.

A9.3 Standard Tacticals.

There are no doubt many useful ways of combining tactics to form larger tactics. We have confined ourselves to just five standard ones, which appear to be especially useful; the utility of others may depend upon the particular tactics which a user defines.

Although we give monotypes below for all these tacticals, their actual types are polymorphic - as you can see from their definitions (which we give for all except $THEN and $THENL); to discover their polytypes you can just say e.g.

> $THEN ;;

to the system. Suffice it to say that they are polymorphic enough that they work for any choice of types for goals and events.

IDTAC : tactic

> This nullary tactical (i.e. tactic) just passes the goal through unchanged.Its principal use is in defining composite tactics and tacticals - see for example REPEAT below. The definition is

> > let IDTAC g = [g], hd ;;

$ORELSE : tactic # tactic -> tactic

> The tactic Tl ORELSE T2 acts on a goal as Tl unless the latter fails, in which case it acts as T2.

> > let $ORELSE(Tl,T2) g = Tl g ? T2 g ;;

$THEN : tactic # tactic -> tactic

> The tactic Tl THEN T2 first applies Tl to the goal, then applies T2 to all the resulting subgoals. Failure if either Tl or T2 fails. We omit its definition; it involves some list-processing both to flatten the list of lists of subgoals into a list of subgoals, and to build the inverse operation into the proof component of the result.

$THENL : tactic # tactic list -> tactic

      The tactic T THENL [T1; ..;Tn] first applies T to the goal,
yielding subgoals [g1; ..;gm] ; if m=n it then applies Ti to gi
respectively, otherwise it fails with `THENL`.

REPEAT : tactic -> tactic

      The tactic REPEAT T applies T repeatedly to the goal and all
subgoals so produced, until T is no longer applicable (i.e.
would fail). REPEAT T never fails.

      letrec REPEAT(T) g = ((T THEN REPEAT(T)) ORELSE IDTAC) g ;;

    Simple examples of composite tactics, using these tacticals, can be
found in Sections 1.1, 3.1.2 and Appendix 1.

Tracing ML functions

Although the ML typechecker will catch many programming errors at compile-time, one's program may still produce spurious results whose explanation is not readily apparent. In ML this is particularly likely when a function fails unexpectedly; the failure is then identified only by a failure token, which may be insufficient for the user to isolate the cause of the error. In such circumstances (and others) it is convenient to be able to trace functions to obtain additional information about their execution.

Rather than catering for a fixed style or mode of tracing (which tends to generate a lot of output, most of which is irrelevant) we describe here an experimental mechanism which gives the user considerable freedom to trace his functions selectively in ways specified by him. This is provided via a system-defined function TRACE, which is a curried function of two arguments: a functional Phi determining how a function is to be modified, and a function f to be traced. When applied to f, the functional Phi is expected to return a pair (f',info) where f' is the modified function and the second component info allows for auxiliary results (usually functions) enabling later access to the tracing information; evaluating TRACE(Phi)(f) overwrites f with f' and returns info as its result. (We shall see how info is used in the examples below).

More precisely, TRACE is defined to have the effect suggested by the ML definition

```
let TRACE Phi f =
        let f',info = Phi f
        in
            f := f' ;
            info    ;;
```

where the assignment is interpreted as overwriting the function value of f with that of f'.

The type of TRACE can now be seen. The function to be traced can be of any function type, so f has type (* -> **). The functional Phi must map f to a function of the same type paired with the auxiliary information which can be of any type ***, and the latter is the result type of TRACE(Phi)(f). So the type of TRACE is given by

TRACE: ((*->**) -> ((*->**) # ***)) -> (*->**) -> ***

A corresponding untracing function

UNTRACE: (*->**) -> bool

is also provided as standard. UNTRACE(f) returns false if f has not been traced, otherwise resets f to the value it had before it was last traced and returns true.

The simplest and most common uses of TRACE arise when one wishes to surround a function with a prelude and a postlude to be executed when the function is entered and exited. The prelude and postlude might be used to output information about the function "on the fly", or to save the tracing information in variables for later inspection. A general format for many tracing functionals in this style is given by

```
let Phi f =
        letref own1, own2, ... = ...
        in
        let f' arg =
                ...% prelude % ... ;
                (let res = f arg
                 in  ...% postlude % ... ;
                        res )
        in
            (f',info)    ;;
```

The letref-declaration here initialises variables for accumulating the tracing information; since their scope is limited to the body of Phi, effectively they serve as <u>own variables</u> of f' (so that different functions traced with the same Phi will use different own variables). External inspection of the accumulated information at any later time is catered for by returning as info suitable functions referring to own1, own2, ... as free variables. For example, if the function (\().own1,own2,...) is returned as info, this then becomes the result of a call TRACE(Phi)(f), so that after

```
let InfoFunction = TRACE Phi f ;;
 . . .
 . . .
```

evaluating InfoFunction() will yield the current values of the own variables.

The following examples illustrate some simple techniques for writing tracing functionals.

Example 1: Counting function calls.

To count how many times a function is applied, one may trace it by the following functional:

```
let CountCalls f =
        letref count = 0
        in
            (\x. count:=count+1 ;   f x ) ,
            (\().count)      ;;
```

This will accumulate a count irrespective of whether a call of f succeeds or fails. Here is a modification which uses different postludes for successful and failing calls, incrementing own variables scount and fcount, respectively; in the failing case, binding the failure token to the trap variable tok ensures that when f fails then f' fails with the same failure token;

```
let CountCalls' f =
        letref scount,fcount = 0,0
        in
        let f' x =
                (let r = f x
                 in  scount := scount+1 ;
                     r
                )?\tok (fcount := fcount+1 ;
                        failwith tok )
        in
            f' , (\().scount,fcount)  ;;
```

As a further refinement, suppose f is a recursive function and one wishes to count only its outermost calls. The following tracing functional will achieve this:

```
let CountTopCalls f =
        letref scount,fcount = 0,0
           and depth = 0
        in
        let f' x =
                depth := depth+1 ;
                (let r = f x
                 in  depth := depth-1 ;
                     if depth=0 then scount := scount+1 ;
                     r
                )?\tok (depth := depth-1 ;
                        if depth=0 then fcount := fcount+1 ;
                        failwith tok )
        in
            f' , (\().scount,fcount)  ;;
```

Note that the failure trap is _necessary_ here, to decrement depth after failure.

Example 2: History variables.

To trace a function of type (ty -> ty') so that its complete history is recorded as a list of ordered pairs, using a disjoint sum for the result component to distinguish between success and failure, one may use

```
let History f =
      letref h = []:(ty # (ty' + tok))list
      in
      let f' x =
            (let r = f x
             in  h := (x,inl(r)).h ;
                 r
            )?\tok (h := (x,inr(tok)).h ;
                       failwith tok  )
      in
          f' , (\().h)    ;;
```

Here, the types ty and ty' must be monotypes and the variable h must
be explicitly monotyped, since an assignment to h occurs within a
\-expression - the body of f' - in the scope of h. [See (2)(i)(b)
in section 2.4.2 and point (4) in the discussion in section 2.4.3.]

Often one doesn't want a complete history, of course, but it is a
straightforward programming exercise to make the addition to counts or
history variables dependent on, say, a predicate of the arguments
and/or results. Here is a simple example along these lines:

Example 3: Debugging revised functions.

Suppose an old version, Oldf, of a function of type (ty -> ty')
which is known to be correct has been rewritten (e.g. for efficiency
reasons) but is producing incorrect results for some arguments.   The
new version, Newf, can be traced to record disagreements with Oldf as
follows, accumulating a list of triples (arg,res,wrong) where res is
the correct result computed by Oldf and wrong is the result computed
by Newf:

```
let BugHistory Oldf Newf =
      letref bugs = []:(ty # ty' # ty')list
      in
      let Newf' x =
            let res = Oldf x
            and res' = Newf x
            in
                if not(res=res') then bugs := (x,res,res').bugs ;
                res
      in
          Newf' , (\().bugs)    ;;

let NewfBugInfoFn = TRACE (BugHistory Oldf) Newf  ;;
```

(For simplicity of exposition, failure of Oldf and/or Newf has been
ignored above but is easily incorporated using disjoint sumtypes and
failure trapping as in example 2.)

Example 4: Entering and exiting messages.

Traditional tracing - printing messages as a function is entered
and exited - is a simple special case:

```
let Messages (entering,exiting,failing) f =
      let f' x =
            entering(x) ;
            (let r = f x
             in  exiting(x,r) ;
                    r
            )?\tok (failing(x,tok) ;
                    failwith tok  )
      in
         f' , ()    ;;
```

where we have parameterised Messages on functions for printing the
entry, success exit and failure messages, in some format appropriate
to the argument and result type of a function to be traced.

Example 5: A tracing functional generator.

Suppose one wishes to count all calls of two functions f and g
using a common counting variable. Then CountCalls as in example 1 is
no use as it generates separate own counting variables for different
functions. A global count could be used but then all functions traced
by the same functional would use this same counting variable.   A
better solution is via a tracing functional generator, making the
count an own variable of the tracing functional, as follows:

```
let SameCountGen () =
      letref count = 0
      in
      let SameCount f =
                  (\x. count := count+1 ;   f x ) ,
                  (\().count)
      in  SameCount  ;;

let TraceWithSameCount (g,h) =
      let SameCount = SameCountGen()
      in
         TRACE SameCount g ;
         TRACE SameCount h       ;;
```

Then after

```
let CountFn1 = TraceWithSameCount(g1,h1)
and CountFn2 = TraceWithSameCount(g2,h2) ;;
```

later evaluation of CountFn1() will return the total number of calls
of g1 and h1, while CountFn2() will return the total number of calls
of g2 and h2.

Apart from debugging, tracing may be used for producing proofs. In normal working with the present LCF system proofs are not stored or displayed at all; only the theorems which are the results of proofs are stored. If one wished to see the proof, one means of doing this is to trace the inference rules so their use is recorded in a list or output to a file. In the most extreme form - by tracing <u>all</u> the basic inference rules - a complete proof in the logician's sense, line-by-line, can be produced. More often, though, one will be content with a more abbreviated proof; in the goal-directed style via tactics, for instance, one might want to modify tactics so that applications of their proof components (i.e. the functions of type thm list -> thm) are recorded in an abbreviated "higher-level" proof-tree. This is quite easy to do with the tracing techniques illustrated above.

Some limitations.

The tracing facility described is less satisfactory than we would like in several respects:

1. Sometimes it is necessary to write several tracing functionals when, in some sense, one should apparently be sufficient. For example, CountCalls in example 1 is intended for functions of a single argument, so if used for a curried function of more than one argument will accumulate a count only of how many times it is applied to a first argument; if one wanted to count how many times a curried function of, say, two arguments is applied to both its arguments, it is necessary to use instead the tracing functional

```
        let CountCalls2 f =
            letref count = 0
            in
                (\x.\y. count := count+1 ;  f x y ) ,
                (\().count)  ;;
```

In a typeless language, CountCalls and CountCalls2 are easily generalised to a tracing functional parameterised on an integer number of arguments for a curried function, but to the best of our knowledge this kind of "polymorphism" - where the result type depends not on the argument <u>type</u> but on the <u>value</u> of a parameter known only at call time - cannot be expressed within the ML type discipline.

2. Not all ML functions are traceable. All user-defined functions will be, but certain system-defined ones are not; attempting to trace the latter will fail, with token `TRACE`, after printing the message

        "CLOSURE NOT TRACEABLE: id"

where id is the name of the function. However, use of such a function can be traced by first rebinding id in ML, i.e. by declaring

```
        let id args = id args ;;
```

before any expression involving a call of id.

3. As the message in 2. indicates, strictly speaking it is not
   functions which are traced but the closures representing them. Thus
   if the same closure is known by two different names, say by
   declaring

```
        let f = \x.--- ;;
        let g = f ;;
```

then tracing calls of f will also trace calls of g, and vice versa.

4. Tracing polymorphic functions can lead to breaches in the security
   of the type system, for there is no way that TRACE can ensure that
   the modified function is at least as polymorphic as the unmodified
   one. It is recommended therefore that only monotyped functions are
   traced (though again the implementation cannot check this, since
   types are not known at run-time).

5. Notice that all ML printing functions are monotyped, and own
   variables, which must clearly be assignable to be of any use, must
   be monotyped to satisfy the typing constraint for letref-bound
   variables occurring free in \-expressions (as in example 2). In
   practice this means that tracing will only be effective for
   monotyped functions in any case (unless the form of tracing one
   wants is independent of a function's arguments and results, such as
   counting function calls or gathering timing statistics).

Some of these limitations can be overcome by making TRACE a
construct of the language, but we have rejected this at least for the
time being for the programming convenience during debugging of having
TRACE available as an ordinary ML function.

The DECsystem-10 Implementation

A11.1 Implementation Details

Edinburgh LCF is implemented in Stanford LISP 1.6 running under TOPS-10 (version 6.03A) on the Edinburgh DECsystem-10. This consists of a DEC KI10 CPU with 256K words of core and 512K words of fixed disk memory (for swapping). The current maximum physical core slot is 75K, and the system (which is about 60K) runs well on non-trivial examples within this. Unfortunately paging causes the system to thrash (because of the well known difficulty of sharing list structures over pages), and so the response with smaller physical core slots would be poor.

A11.2 Getting into ML

The following illustrates an entry into ML:

```
*----------------------------------------------------------*
|                                                          |
|     .RUN LCF                                             |
|                                                          |
|     *(TML)                                              |
|                                                          |
|     Edinburgh LCF                                        |
|                                                          |
|     THEORY?                                              |
|                                                          |
|     DRAFT?                                               |
|                                                          |
|     #                                                    |
|                                                          |
*----------------------------------------------------------*
```

Notes:

1. One starts by running the appropriate core-image (called LCF above).

2. On entering LCF the system prompts with "*"; one is now in LISP.

3. To enter ML one types "(TML)<return>". The system will respond with "THEORY?" and one should then reply either "T<return>", if one wants to work in an existing theory named "T" (see 3.4), or just <return> (as above) if one doesn't want to work in a theory. In the second case, the system

will respond with "DRAFT?"; and one should then reply either "D<return>", to work in a new (or existing) draft named "D", or just "<return>" (as above) if one wants to work in a nameless draft - that is, one doesn't want to preserve ones results for later use.

4. Finally one recieves the ML prompt "#".

A11.3 Interacting with ML

When talking at top-level to ML one can evaluate expressions, perform declarations or begin and end sections (see Chapter 2). At any time the input buffer can be cleared back to the last ";;" by typing "CTRL-D<return>", for example:

```
#let fact n = if n=0 th↑D

#letrec fact n = if n=0 then 1 else n*fact(n-1);;
fact = - : (int -> int)
```

To get from ML to LISP one types "CTRL-G"; to get from LISP to ML one types "(TML)<return>" again (one only recieves the THEORY? and DRAFT? prompts after the first call of TML). This is occasionally necessary since ML fails to trap certain errors, putting you unexpectedly in LISP.

```
#9999999999999999;;

INTEGER OVERFLOW

*(TML)

#
```

To get from ML to monitor level one should first go to LISP with "CTRL-G", and then exit to the monitor by typing "CTRL-C". After such an exit the core-image may by saved on disk using the "SAVE" monitor command; it may subsequently be run using the "RUN" command. WARNING: Due to bugs in Stanford LISP, reentered core-images occasionally develop strange properties!

A11.4 Increasing Core Size

To increase the core size of a job one does the following:

1. Exit to monitor-level ("CTRL-G" then "CTRL-C").

2. Execute a "CORE" monitor command (e.g. "CORE 100" to increase core size to 100).

3. Reenter LISP by typing "REE<return>".

4. Reenter ML by typing "(TML)<return>".

BIBLIOGRAPHY

Logical background. The main inspiration for our project came from Dana Scott with his work on continuous functions. The model theory of PPLAMBDA - given in the Arc-et-Senans conference paper cited later - is based on:

   D.S.Scott, "Lattice theoretic models for various type-free calculi", Proc 4th International Congress in Logic, Methodology and the Philosophy of Science, Bucharest (1972).

while PPLAMBDA itself is a natural deduction system developed from his typed \-calculus with an induction rule (later known as fixed-point induction), reported in an unpublished paper (1969). An early formulation of this rule occurs in:

   D.M.R.Park, "Fixpoint Induction and Proofs of Program Properties", Machine Intelligence 5 (editors: B.meltzer and D.Michie), American Elsevier, New York (1970).

for a tutorial description, see:

   R.Bird, "Programs and Machines; an introduction to the theory of computation", Wiley (1976).

and a detailed study of formulae for which the rule is valid (see section 3.3) is:

   S.Igarashi, "Admissibility of fixed-point induction in first order logic of typed theories", Memo AIM-168, Stanford University (1972).

For a definitive exposition of natural deduction, see:

   D.Prawitz, "Natural deduction", Proc 2nd Scandinavian Logic Symposium, ed Fenstad, North Holland (1971).

LCF studies. Work with the predecessor of our LCF system, implemented at Stanford in 1971-2, is reported in:

   L.Aiello, M.Aiello and R.Weyhrauch, "The semantics of PASCAL in LCF", Memo AIM-221, Stanford (1974).

   ---, "PASCAL in LCF: semantics and examples of proof", Theoretical Computer Science 5, pp.135-177 (1977).

   F.W.von Henke, "Recursive data types and program structures", Internal report, GMD, Bonn (1976).

R.Milner, "Logic for Computable Functions: description of a machine implementation", Memo AIM-169, Stanford (1972).

---, "Implementation and application of Scott's logic for computable functions", Proc ACM Conference on Proving Assertions about Programs, SIGPLAN notices 7,1 (1972).

--- and R.Weyhrauch, "Proving compiler correctness in a mechanized Logic", Machine Intelligence 7, ed Michie, Edinburgh University Press (1972).

M.Newey, "Formal semantics of LISP with applications to program correctness", PhD Thesis, Stanford (1975).

---, "Axioms and theorems for integers, lists and finite sets in LCF", Memo AIM-184, Stanford (1973).

R.Weyhrauch and R.Milner, "Program semantics and correctness in a mechanized logic", Proc USA-Japan Computer Conference, Tokyo (1972).

An interesting development from Stanford LCF is:

L.Aiello et. al., "PPC (Pisa Proof Checker): a tool for experiments in theory of proving and mathematical theory of computation", Fundamenta Informaticae 1 (1977).

Edinburgh LCF is reported in:

R.Milner, L.Morris and M.Newey, "A Logic for Computable Functions with reflexive and polymorphic types", LCF Report 1, Computer Science Dept, Edinburgh, and Proc Conference on Proving and Improving Programs, Arc-et-Senans (1975).

M.Gordon, R.Milner, L.Morris, M.Newey and C.Wadsworth, "A metalanguage for interactive proof in LCF", Fifth ACM SIGACT-SIGPLAN Conference on Principles of Programming Languages, Tucson, Arizona (1978).

and illustrations of the tactical approach to proof may be found in:

R.Milner, "Program semantics and mechanized proof", Proc 2nd Advanced Course on Foundations of Computer Science, Mathematical Centre, Amsterdam (1976).

---, "LCF: a methodology for performing rigorous proofs about programs", Proc 1st IBM Symposium on Mathematical Foundations of Computer Science, Amagi, Japan (1976).

---, "LCF: a way of doing proofs with a machine", Proc. 8th MFCS Symposium, Olomouc, Czechoslovakia (1979).

A.J.Cohn, "High Level Proof in LCF", Proc. 4th Workshop on Automated Deduction, Austin, Texas (1979).

---, PhD Thesis, Edinburgh (1979).

D.A.Giles, "The Theory of Lists in LCF", Report CSR-31-78, Computer Science Dept., Edinburgh University (1978).

Proof Methodology. A source of much work on theorem proving in the Predicate Calculus, is:

J.A.Robinson, "A machine-oriented logic based on the resolution principle", JACM 12,1 (1965).

Fixed strategies for proofs by structural induction are described in:

R.S.Boyer and J.S.Moore, "Proving theorems about LISP functions", JACM 22,1 (1975).

R.Aubin, "Mechanizing structural induction", PhD Thesis, Edinburgh University (1976).

Pure proof-checking - in which the machine is: supplied with the whole proof - is exemplified most fully by the work of de Bruijn and his group at Eindhoven; it achieved notable success in the translation and validation of a standard mathematical text:

L.S.van Benthem Jutting, "Checking Landau's `Grundlagen` in the AUTOMATH system", Thesis, Technische Hogeschool, Eindhoven (1977).

An example of a system in which one may design proof strategies, though without any security against faulty deduction, is:

C.Hewitt, "PLANNER: a language for manipulating models and proving theorems in a robot", AI Memo 168, Project MAC, M.I.T. (1970).

Other approaches (of which the first three are specialised to proofs about programs) are:

R.L.Constable and M.J.O'Donnell, "A Programming Logic", Winthrop (1978).

V.R.Pratt, "Semantical considerations of Floyd-Hoare logic", Proc. 17th Annual IEEE Symposium on Foundations of Computer Science (1976).

H.Rasiowa, "Algorithmic Logic", Inst. of Computer Science, Polish Academy of Sciences, Warsaw (1977).

R.W.Weyhrauch, "Prolegomena to a theory of formal reasoning", Memo
AIM-315, Computer Science Dept., Stanford University (1978).

Background to ML. Functional programming languages which influenced
the design of ML are reported in:

R.M.Burstall and R.Popplestone, "POP-2 reference manual", Machine
Intelligence 2, ed Dale and Michie, Oliver and Boyd (1968).

A.Evans, "PAL: a language designed for teaching programming
linguistics", Proc ACM 23rd National Conference, Brandin
Systems Press, Princeton, NJ (1968).

P.J.Landin, "The next 700 programming languages", Comm ACM 9,3
(1966).

J.C.Reynolds, "GEDANKEN: a simple typeless programming language
based on the principle of completeness and the reference
concept", Comm ACM 13,5 (1970).

For the development of the notion of abstract type in programming,
see:

R.M.Burstall and J.A.Goguen, "Putting theories together to make
specifications"", Proc. 5th International Conference on
Artificial Intelligence, Cambridge Mass., published by the
Dept. Comp. Sci., Carnegie Mellon (1977).

O.-J.Dahl et al, "The SIMULA 67 common base language", Norwegian
Computing Centre, Oslo (1968).

J.V.Guttag, "The specification and application to programming of
abstract data types", PhD Thesis, University of Toronto
(1975).

B.H.Liskov and S.Zilles, "Programming with abstract data types",
Proc Symposium on Very High-level Languages, SIGPLAN notices
9,4 (1974).

B.H.Liskov et.al., "Abstraction Mechanisms in CLU", Comm ACM 20,8
(1977).

R.A.Wulf, R.L.London and M.Shaw, "Abstraction and verification in
ALPHARD: introduction to language and methodology",
Carnegie-Mellon University (1976).

S.Zilles, "Algebraic specification of data types", Computation
Structures Group Memo 119, M.I.T. (1974).

The notion of a polymorphic type discipline is discussed in the following papers (Strachey appears to be the first to have seen the various possibilities and difficulties):

C.Strachey, "Fundamental concepts in programming languages", unpublished notes for NATO Summer School, Copenhagen (1967).

D.Gries and N.Gehani, "Some ideas on data types in high-level languages", Comm ACM 20,6 (1977).

The theory supporting polymorphism in ML is expounded in:

R.Milner, "A Theory of Type Polymorphism in Programming", Journal of Computer and System Sciences 17 (1978).

An expository account of functional programming (but without the benefit of an explicit type discipline) can be found in:

W.H.Burge, "Recursive Programming Techniques", Addison-Wesley, Reading, Mass. (1975).

Finally, for a discussion of an interesting style of programming that is naturally accomodated within ML, see:

J.Backus, "Can Programming Be Liberated from the von Neumann Style? A Functional Style and its Algebra of Programs", Comm ACM 21,8 (1978).

INDEX